FRIENDS OF ASTORIA COLUMN

PRESERVATION, STEWARSHIP AND PUBLIC EDUCTION

Within three years of the Column's completion in 1926, the ravages of 80 inches of rainfall a year and the driving gale winds sweeping off the Pacific Ocean dimmed the beauty and threatened the carvings on the great spiraling mural of history.

Years passed and the mural continued to deteriorate, faded and worn by time, despite efforts to protect it.

A chance meeting in 1984 between the Astoria Mayor, Edith Henningsgaard, and Jordan Schnitzer, a Portland philanthropist with roots in Astoria, spurred determination to save the Column.

By 1988 a rescue plan was created and the Friends of Astoria Column was launched. Inspired by the potential loss of history, the Friends raised $1 million and retained world-renowned conservator, Frank Preusser who had also worked on the Sphinx in Egypt.

As the work began, it was estimated that only 20% of the original art remained. After two years, the grand opening was held in late 1995.

Building on their initial success, the Friends undertook a $2 million project in 2005 adding visitor improvements and the stunning act of lighting the Column.

In 2007, an annual inspection found cracks in the staircase after the wear and tear of 400,000 annual visitors. Once again, a fund-raising campaign was introduced and the Friends managed one of the most complex projects ever undertaken.

Central to the Friends success has been the thousands of small and large contributions from all over the world. Because the Column calls us to keep sharing its stories, please join with the Friends as they continue their stewardship and commitment to one of history's most treasured monuments.

For inquiries about merchandise, contributions and information, please contact
www.AstoriaColumn.org

ASTORIA COLUMN · DEDICATED 1926

ASTORIA OREGON USA

1811 ASTORIA BICENTENNIAL 2011

Contents

Art Contest Winner by Ted Vaught

95

Astoria Bicentennial Committees

Executive Committee

Edith Henningsgaard – Miller, Honorary Chair
Vernon Fowler, Co-Chair
Jean K. Harrison, Co-Chair
Paulette Hankel McCoy, Director, Astoria Bicentennial
McAndrew Burns, Executive Director, Clatsop County Historical Society

Steering Committee
Dick Basch
McAndrew Burns
A. Diane Collier
Bruce Conner
Sarah Englund
Brett Estes
Terry Finklein
James M. Flint (†2009)
Cheri J. Folk
Vernon & Nancy Fowler
Rae Goforth
Jean K. Harrison
John Goodenberger
Skip Hauke
Blair Henningsgaard
Cindy Howe
Lynn Jackson
Arline LaMear
Joseph Leahy
Larry Lockett
Paulette McCoy
Edith Henningsgaard Miller
Donna Quinn
Pat Roscoe
June Spence
Thane Tienson

Education
Larry Lockett, Co-Chair
Stephen Schoonmaker, Co-Chair
McAndrew Burns
Betsey Ellerbroek
John Goodenberger
Matt Hensley
Lynn Jackson
Patrick Kane
Paulette McCoy
Cathy Peterson
Betty Satterwhite

Marketing Media
Donna Quinn, Co-Chair
Paula Bue
Laura Guimond
Paulette McCoy, Co-Chair
Patricia Hankel Nelson
Rex Ziak

Merchandise
Paula Bue
Sarah Englund
Cindy Howe
Jennifer Johnson
Paulette McCoy
Pat Roscoe

Legacy
Arline LaMear, Chair
Pam Alegria
McAndrew Burns
Michael Foster
Blair Henningsgaard
Mitch Mitchum
Paulette McCoy
June Spence

Opening Event
Cheri J. Folk, Chair
Terry Finklein, Vice Chair
Devon D. Abing
Doiniscio Abing
Rosemary Baker-Monaghan
Bruce Conner
LTJG Stephen J. Drauszewski
Brett Estes
Vernon & Nancy Fowler
Capt. Douglas E. Kaup
Paulette McCoy
Cyndi Mudge
Dave Pearson
Norman Shatto
LTJG Zachary R. Vojtech
LTJG Adam M. Whalen

Heritage Festival
Cyndi Mudge, Chair
Nancy Anderson
Calvin & Agnes Brown
A. Diane Collier
Rae Goforth
Jean Harrison
Dea Helligso
Norma Hermandez
Loran Mathews
Helen Pitkanen
Leena Riker
Gerry Swenson
Shirley Tinner

Admiral's Ball
Jan Van Dusen, Chair
Steve Buckelew
Bruce Conner
Sarah Englund
Liz Knutsen
Paulette McCoy
Al Olson
Carol Olson
Eric Paulson, Regatta President

Super Homecoming Committee

Joseph Leahy, Chair
Laura Bredleau
Jane Donnelly, Jeff Donnelly,
    Fur Trade Encampment Chairs
Mike Goin
William J. Hankel
Jeanette Sampson
Chris Stangland
Rick Williams

Fundraising

McAndrew Burns
The Honorable Betsy Johnson
Paulette McCoy
Mike Sorkki
Thane Tienson

Upriver Fundraiser Party, Portland Yacht Club

Presented by the Friends of the Astoria Coumn,

President, Jordan D. Schnitzer
Trudy Van Dusen Citovic, Event Coordinator
Host Committee Byron Beck & Juan Martinez
Robert Bishop III & Carolyn Bishop
Harry and Shirley Braunstein
John Brodie & Blair Saxon- Hill
Djordje & Trudy Van Dusen Citovic
Connie Dalla Gasperina
Lori Flex & Jeff Sackett
Michael Foster
Laura Guimond & Pete Petersen
The Honorable Betsy Johnson
Helena B. Lankton
Mike & Carolyn Lindberg
Edith Henningsgaard Miller
Eric Paulson
Cheryl Perrin
Jordan D. Schnitzer
Ruth Shaner
Harold & Jeanyse Snow

Thane Tienson
Ron & Gayle Timmerman
Mayor Willis L. Van Dusen
Karen Whitman & Brad Shiley
Donna Quinn

An Adventure in History Program

Bryan Penttila, Editor
Rick Anderson, Art Director

Printed in Oregon

Copyright © 2010, Clatsop County Historical Society, Inc. All rights reserved. No part of this publication may be reproduced, stored in a retrieval system or transmitted, in any form or by any means, electronic, mechanical, photocopying, recording, or otherwise, without the prior written permission of the publisher.

Published by Clatsop County Historical Society, Inc.
714 Exchange Street, P.O. Box 88
Astoria, Oregon 97103

Thank you to our Sponsors

John Jacob Astor Society $50,000 plus

City of Astoria Promote Astoria Fund

Mayor Willis L. Van Dusen

Councilors: Blair Henningsgaard, Arline LaMear, Peter Roscoe, Russ Warr, City Manager Paul Benoit

Astoria School District 1 C *(Teacher's In Service Day)* • Clatsop County Historical Society • Fort Stevens State Park *(Site for Fur- Trade Encampment)*

Astoria Empire Builder $25,000 - $49,999

Pacific Power

Astoria Salmon King $10,000 - $24,999
Bank of Astoria
Bumble Bee Foods, Inc.
Columbia Memorial Hospital
Fort George Brewery & Public House
Friends of the Astoria Column, Inc.
NW Natural
Oregon Community Foundation
Oregon Heritage Commission
Don Vallaster

Astoria Timber Baron $5,000 - $9,999
Astoria Regatta Association
Bornstein's Seafood
Cannery Pier Hotel
Columbia River Maritime Museum
Englund Marine & Industrial Supply
Samuel S. Johnson Foundation
Lum's Auto Dealership
Snow Family Foundation

Astoria Heritage Circle $1,000 - $4,999
Banker's Suite & Ballroom
Columbia River Bar Pilots

Georgia Pacific Wauna Mill
Steve Forrester & Brenda Penner
Paul Gillum
Rae Goforth
Tom & Alice Gustafson
George & Jean Harrison
Edith Henningsgaard Miller
Joseph & Judy Leahy
Liberty Theater Restoration
Lee & Paulette McCoy
Donna Quinn
Sterling Savings Bank
Sunset Empire Transportation
Van Dusen Family
Walldorf (Germany) Winery
Wet Dog Cafe & Brewery
Whole Brain Creative

Voyageur $500 - $999
Columbia River Business Journal
Daily Astorian
Del & Cheri Folk
Vern & Nancy Fowler
Gimre's Shoes
Holiday Inn Express Hotel & Suites- Astoria

Polk Riley Printing & Design
Thane Tienson
Tongue Point Job Corps Center

Fur Trader $200 - $499
Anonymous Homesick Astorian
Astoria Music Festival
Baked Alaska Restaurant
McAndrew & René Burns
Terry & Chris Finklein
Fulio's Pastaria, Tuscan Steak House and Deli
Evelyn Leahy Hankel
Kathleen Hudson
John & Sandra Kalander
Jerry & Jane Kirkpatrick
Knutsen Insurance
Clifford & Arline LaMear
Bob & Gayle Landwehr
William J. Leahy Council 1307 KNIGHTS OF COLUMBUS
Luottamus Partners
Old Town Framing
Alfred & Carol Olson
Leena Mela Riker
Sundial Travel & Cruise Center
Holly McHone Jewelry

PROUD TO BE THE BANK OF ASTORIA.

Bank of Astoria has been a part of your coastal community for over 40 years, we know about the rewards (and challenges) of living here. Whatever the size of your company–and whatever your financial goals for the future–the team at Bank of Astoria is here to help you.

We are pleased to be Salmon King Sponsors of the Astoria Bicentennial celebration.

Bank of **Astoria**

Now. And for the voyage ahead.

503.325.2228
www.BankofAstoria.com

ASTORIA
1811~2011
AN ADVENTURE IN HISTORY©

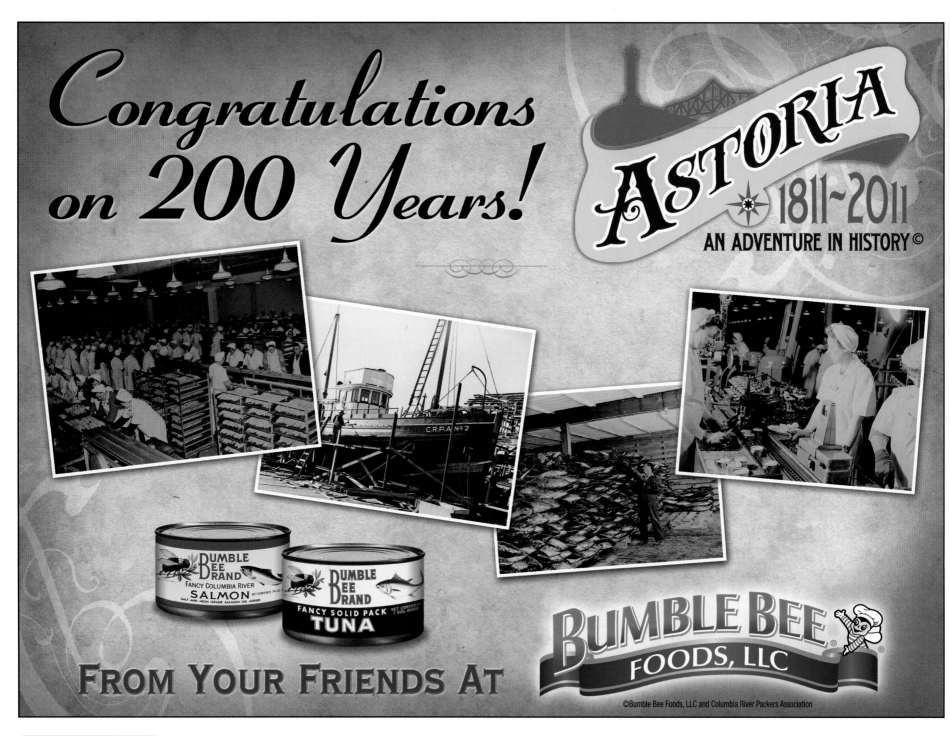

Committed to your health care for 130 years & beyond

At **Columbia Memorial Hospital**, we are honored that so many have chosen us to provide their health care needs. We are proud of our heritage and service to the North Coast and look forward to many more years of service.

Columbia Memorial Hospital evolved from the region's first hospital, St. Mary's Hospital, established in 1880.

In 1919, the Astoria Finnish Brotherhood began a second facility, Columbia Hospital. The Augustana Lutheran Church took over the project and the hospital opened in 1927.

In 1971, St. Mary's Hospital was purchased by Columbia Hospital. In the mid-70's, the hospital trustees approved a new site and plan.

Columbia Memorial Hospital, a Lutheran-Affiliated Healthcare Facility, was founded and opened in 1977.

We are a not-for-profit, community-based hospital, one of only four remaining in the state of Oregon.

We are excited about the future of the hospital and we are busy building that future with new additions, such as our new CMH-OHSU Cancer and Cardiology Centers and our surgery renovation project.

Columbia Memorial Hospital — building the future for the next generation of lower Columbia residents.

COLUMBIA MEMORIAL HOSPITAL
body+mind+spirit
A Lutheran-Affiliated Healthcare Facility

2111 EXCHANGE ST. • ASTORIA, OREGON
503-325-4321
www.columbiamemorial.org

Welcome to Astoria

It's our birthday. We are celebrating 200 years of Astoria's history. Our historic town was founded 48 years before our State of Oregon. We were established before the cities of San Francisco, Portland and Seattle. Madison was President, Napoleon was in France, and John Jacob Astor was dreaming of a nation that stretched from the Atlantic to the Pacific. John Jacob Astor's little settlement was the first claim to making that dream come true. A lot has happened during the past two centuries.

Astor's fur-trading party carved out a small settlement along the banks of the mighty river of the West, the Columbia. Immigrants have been coming ever since. The British came during the War of 1812. Finns, Swedes, Norwegians, and others came to fish and work in the forests. As Astoria became the "canning capitol of the world" Chinese came to work in the canneries. In the pages that follow, you're going to read about these groups and others who have made Astoria what it is today. But, I hope you'll do more than just read about our history . . . come and experience it firsthand.

Our history comes alive here. We've got a world-class maritime museum. Take the time to see our beautiful, breathtaking, view from the Astoria Column. We are proud of our Victorian architecture. The community has restored our beautiful Liberty Theater. Recently, in 2010, we opened a brand new museum in the historic "Goonies Jail" that celebrates all of the Hollywood movies that have been filmed here. My favorite is a working trolley, built in 1913 that runs along our river walk.

We have great hotels, bed and breakfasts, and restaurants. Our walkable, historic downtown is filled with shops you'll

love—including a JC Penny and a Sears. I challenge you to find a community our size with both in a downtown setting.

Many of you are going to fall in love with Astoria because of what our history offers. But I am most proud of the people who live here. We are a town where people say hello to each other on the street, happily give directions and suggestions to make your visit as great as possible. We've been sharing our town with visitors for two hundred years, and we're ready to share it with you.

We're two hundred years old and we're throwing a birthday party and you're invited! Have a great time.

Willis L. Van Dusen

Mayor City of Astoria

The first American settlement west of the Rocky Mountains welcomes you with open arms to our Bicentennial Celebration. While Astoria has changed significantly since the Lewis & Clark Expedition and the John Jacob Astor party arrived, we have many unique and fascinating cultural treasurers to share with you.

First and foremost, the magnificent Columbia River that so clearly defines our unique Sense of Place; the Astoria Column at the top of the Coxcomb Hill that chronicles our history from Captain Robert Gray to the Lewis & Clark Expedition and beyond. The historic Flavel House and Heritage Museum; and our wonderful Maritime Museum celebrate the story of just how the River and the Sea shaped this place we call home. All you have to do is look at the Victorian and Craftsman homes dotting the hills of Astoria to realize what a great place this is. It has long been said that Astoria is a "Little San Francisco." But it would seem to me, since Astoria came first, San Francisco is really just a "Big Astoria."

We come from a hearty stock of diverse ancestors: the Scandinavians who contributed so much to shaping our community and our cultural traditions and the Chinese who literally built Astoria (both times—before and after the Great Fire of 1922). We value the contributions of the Hawaiians and we must give special tribute to the Native Americans who welcomed our ancestors, especially the great Clatsop-Nehalem Tribe who helped the Lewis & Clark Expedition survive their long winter at Fort Clatsop.

Take the time to stroll along our beautiful river walk and you will feel the creative pulse of Astoria. We are a vibrant, diverse community: our growing senior population attracted to our community because of our commitment and interest in education and life-long learning; young, creative adults settling here to build a great life for their families; the canneries and great restaurants and places to sit and enjoy the incredible summer sunsets along the river. We are a community of people full of life, honoring the best of who we have been, embracing the fullness of who we are now, and anticipating the most of who we can become.

Our August Regatta dates from 1894, making it the oldest festival in the Pacific Northwest. Our Farmers Market in the spring/summer/fall, the Fisher Poets Festival in February, the Crab and Wine Festival in April, Music Festival and Scandinavian Festival in mid-June all highlight our creative gathering place of events that make Astoria a destination for so many people in the Northwest. And don't forget to ride the Trolley!

If it sounds like I'm proud of my community, you are correct. If you visit us and you don't get to experience everything the first time, you'll just have to make plans to come back. And when you do, we will

welcome you with open arms again. After all, that's what we have been doing for 200 years—welcoming visitors to Astoria with open arms. And that is something worth celebrating!

Edith Henningsgaard Miller
Honorary Chair Astoria Bicentennial

JANUARY 27, 2011

Adventure in History Lecture Series "The Russian Exploration of the Northern Pacific, 1741-1823", featuring Mark Eifler, professor of history at University of Portland, speaker and author of two books. Evening includes music performed by Con Amici Chamber Players, dessert bar and beverages, lecture and book signing.

7 p.m., Liberty Theater, Astoria.

VIEW OF ASTORIA, OREGON.

FEBRUARY 19, 2011

Tears of Joy Puppet Theater presents "The Bridge of the Gods" This play is based on a Klickitat version of the legend and is written by Native American storyteller Ed Edmo, designed by Lillian Pitt and poetry by Elizabeth Woody. (An early adaptation of this tale was created and performed as a musical event at Astoria's 1911 Centennial.)

7 p.m., Liberty Theater, Astoria.

APRIL 12, 2011

Adventure in History Lecture Series "The Astor Party and the Founding of Astoria; Why It Matters to the Nation", featuring Rex Ziak, local historian, author, filmmaker, publisher, photographer and Emmy Award recipient. Evening includes music performed by Brownsmead Flats, dessert bar, beverages, lecture and book signing.

7 p.m., Liberty Theater, Astoria.

APRIL 29, 30 May 1, 2011

Crab, Seafood & Wine Festival – Enjoy Oregon wine, local beers, seafood and other delectable food items while exploring over 200 vendor booths of art, jewelry, photography, clothing and other unique gifts.

(Astoria-Warrenton Chamber of Commerce Event)
Clatsop County Fairgrounds

Opening Celebration & Astoria Downtown Birthday Party May 19, 20, 21, 22, 2011

Thursday, May 19

Adventure in History Lecture Series "Astor's Empire" featuring James P. Ronda, H.G. Barnard Professor of Western American History, Emeritus, author of over a dozen published essays and books including "Astoria & Empire" (1990). Evening includes prelude music performed by Con Amici Chamber Players, dessert bar and beverages, lecture and book signing.

7 p.m., Liberty Theater, 12th and Commercial Streets, Astoria.

Friday, May 20

Museum Exhibits Opening Receptions

"200 Years of Art in Astoria Private Collection of Astorian Michael Foster" – (Temporary Exhibit) Mr. Foster is a well-known philanthropist and collector whose 6,000 plus works range from fine art to rare toys. This exhibit will feature Michael's selected favorites that have a tie to Astoria's Bicentennial.

5 p.m. – 8 p.m., Heritage Museum, 16th & Exchange Streets, Astoria. Free Admission, donations accepted.

"Cleveland Rockwell Fine Art Exhibit." – (Temporary Exhibit) Featuring the works of Cleveland Rockwell (1837-1907) one of the foremost painters of the Pacific Northwest. These works are on loan from the Oregon Historical Society, private collections and museums from the Pacific NW.

5 p.m. – 8 p.m., Columbia River Maritime Museum, 17th and Marine Drive, Astoria. Free Admission, donations accepted.

"Astor Party & the Founding of Astoria" This dynamic new exhibit will tell the story of John Jacob Astor, the fur trade, the Astor fur trading party, the Tonquin, Fort George, and the War of 1812.

5 p.m. – 8 p.m., Heritage Museum, Clatsop County Historical Society, 16th & Exchange Streets, Astoria. Free Admission, donations accepted.

Chinook Nation and other Native Tribes Cultural Performance

Members from the Cathlamet, Clatsop, Lower Chinook, Wahkiakum, and Willapa Tribes of the Chinook Nation will sing and perform dancing & drumming accompanied by their friends and relations from the Grande Ronde and Shoalwater Nations in full regalia. Jerry Chapman Aboriginal Band will perform during the second half of the show. Lobby will display two styles of sacred Chinook canoes. Handmade Chinookan arts and crafts will be available for purchase.

7 p.m., Liberty Theater, 12th & Commercial Streets, Astoria.

Saturday, May 21

9:30 a.m. Heritage Fair celebrating Astoria's cultural diversity with food booths, demonstrations, music, dance performances, arts & crafts, weaving, and family friendly events. Located at the Sunset Empire Transit Center Parking Lot, on Marine Drive Between 9th, 10th Astor & Bond Streets.

9:30 a.m. – 5:00 p.m.

11:30 p.m. Historic Trade Re-enactment Ceremony in the Columbia River with the Chinook Tribe and other NW Indian Tribe canoes with the Tall Ships, Lady Washington and Hawaiian Chieftain.

12:15 p.m. Chinese Dragon dancers and Japanese Taiko drummers lead the way along the Columbia Riverwalk to the official opening ceremony at Columbia River Maritime Museum 17th Street Plaza Music. Performances by Astoria High School band and choirs, North Coast Chorale, and other local music groups.

1 p.m. F-15 Fighter Jets Fly-over Portland Air National Guard, Color Guard presented by USGC Columbia River Sector

Official Welcome & Opening Ceremony Presentation — The Honorable Willis L. Van Dusen with State and National Leaders. Birthday Cake & Refreshments

2 p.m. – 5 p.m. Tall Ship tours, Heritage Fair continues, horse and wagon rides, museum exhibits, ride the Old 300 Riverfront Trolley or climb the Astoria Column

2:15 p.m. Chinook Tribe & other NW Tribes canoe races

3: 30 p.m. USCG Search and Rescue Demonstration on the Columbia River. Viewing from 17th Plaza or Riverwalk.

7 p.m. The Land of the Dragon, A Chinese Fantasy Tale written by Madge Miller Family fun for all ages, The Land of the Dragon is a delightful, stylized Chinese play about the captive Princess Jade Pure, the hero, a roving minstrel named Road Wanderer and his dancing pet dragon. Liberty Theater 12th & Commercial Streets, Astoria. Tickets available at the Box Office.

Sunday, May 22

Sunday Market, 10 a.m. – 3 p.m., 12th Street Downtown Astoria, Museum exhibits open, historic tours, Hollywood Film location tours, Schoolhouse Quilter's Exhibit

JUNE 17-26, 2011

Ninth Annual Astoria Music Festival

American, European and Chinese classical music performed by the Festival Orchestra, soloists and other musicians from Astoria's Sister City, Walldorf, Germany under the direction of Festival Artistic Director and Conductor, Keith Clark. Liberty Theater and other Historic Astoria Venues.

JUNE 17-19, 2011

Astoria's 44th Annual Midsummer Scandinavian Festival

Clatsop County Fairgrounds

JULY 2011

July 3 North Coast Symphonic Band Free Concert of familiar and favorite patriotic music. The North Coast Symphonic Band will present a concert of familiar and patriotic music to celebrate a Bicentennial 4th of July in Astoria. A special highlight will be the premiere of a newly commissioned work for wind band written especially to commemorate Astoria's 200th birthday.

7 p.m., Liberty Theater 12th & Commercial Streets, Astoria.

July 4 Enjoy Old Fashion 4th in Downtown Astoria and Riverfront, Fireworks at dusk.

July 15 David Thompson Canoeing Expedition Arrives in Astoria after six weeks of navigating the Columbia River from the British Columbia source to the mouth (Thompson's 200th Anniversary arrival in Astoria, July 15, 1811) Welcome picnic at the train depot.

July 16 Tiller's Folly - Canadian Celtic Concert in honor of Thompson Canoeing Brigade, Liberty Theater, 7:30 p.m. Tickets available at the box office.

Astoria 117th Regatta Festival
AUGUST 10- 14, 2011

Wednesday, August 10

6:00 p.m. Kiddies Parade

Thursday, August 11

7 p.m. Regatta Queen's Coronation & Reception following, Liberty Theater

Friday, August 12

11 a.m. Memorial Park Ceremony
Noon   NW Natural BBQ
2 p.m. Rose Planting, Flavel House Gardens
6 p.m. Admiral's Reception (by Invitation)

Saturday, August 13

9 a.m. Jet Ski Races
Noon   Grand Bicentennial Parade with Honored Guest
        Lord Astor of Hever
2 p.m. Salmon Barbeque
7 p.m. Admiral's Bicentennial Ball aboard Portland Spirit
8 p.m. Blue Jean Bash, Shipyard Inn
10 p.m. Fireworks

Sunday, August 14, 2011

11 a.m. – 3 p.m. Sunday Market, Astoria Downtown on 12th Street
3 p.m.   Outdoor Concert

Astoria Super Homecoming
September 14-18, 2011

Daily Activities

Museum Exhibits at Heritage Museum, Oregon Film Museum, Flavel House, Columbia River Maritime Museum, historic home tours, Hollywood film location tours, climb the Astoria Column, or ride the Riverfront Trolley.

Fur Trade Encampment, 1800-1840 historic reenactment,
Fort Stevens State Park (Historical Park area) Warrenton

Daily, 10 a.m. – 5 p.m. Parking fee

6 p.m. Football game, Class reunion gatherings.

10 a.m. - 5 p.m. Astoria Air Show: "Celebrating 100 Years of Naval Aviation" USCG Air Station, Warrenton

10 a.m. - 5 p.m. Commercial Fishermen's Festival - Meet the crew of the Deadliest Catch and Axe Men while they compete in fishing and logging contests. Enjoy food, music, and fun for the whole family.

The Fur Traders Encampment will represent a living history reenactment to commemorate the establishment of the first permanent American settlement in the Pacific NW by the Pacific Fur Company in 1811. Living history actors will represent not only the members of John Jacob's Astor company, but others involved in the fur trade in the Columbia region from the arrival of the first American party in 1811 to the end of the period of joint British-American occupancy of the Oregon Country in 1846. Demonstrations of fur trading, period crafts and activities will be an important part of the encampment and will include period music or other entertainment.

7:30 p.m. Judy Collins Concert, Liberty Theater 12th & Commercial Streets, Astoria. Tickets available at the Box Office.

11 a.m. – 3 p.m. Sunday Market, Astoria Downtown on 12th Street

2:30 p.m. - Judy Collins Concert, Liberty Theater 12th & Commercial Streets, Astoria. Tickets available at the Box Office

Adventure in History Lecture Series Jane Kirkpatrick, author of sixteen books will tell the incredible story of Madame Marie Dorion, the Iowan Indian women that journeyed with her husband and two small children over the Rockies with the overland Astor Party led by Wilson Price Hunt that arrived in Astoria January 1812. This evening's presentation is based on three historical fiction novels on the life of Marie Dorion: A Name of Her Own, Every Fixed Star and Hold Tight the Thread. Evening includes prelude music performed by World Flute Master, Gary Stroutsos, a dessert bar, beverages, lecture and book signing.

7 p.m., Liberty Theater 12th & Commercial Streets, Astoria.

See these websites:
www.astoria200.org, oldoregon.com
for the full 2011 calendar of community activities
and events.

Reconstructing *Astoria*

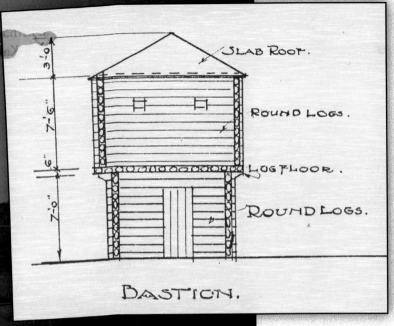

SLAB ROOF.

ROUND LOGS.

LOG FLOOR.

ROUND LOGS.

BASTION.

Architect John E. Wicks and the Centennial Celebration of 1911

By John E. Goodenberger

As Astoria's centennial celebration loomed, city fathers puzzled over how to rightly honor Astor's men and the settlement's birth. Flush with civic spirit, Astorians turned to Finnish-American architect John E. Wicks to design a replica of the stockade and blockhouses that comprised the original "Astoria." But the memorial did not last. Like the original structure, it succumbed to the damp local climate and was toppled with a good shove. Fifty years later the city would turn once again to Wicks for help in reconstructing "Astoria."

"Uncle" Job Ross was the first person to wreak havoc on Astoria's original landmark, or at least he was the first to brag about it. Born in 1811,

the same year Astor's trading post at the mouth of the Columbia River was built, his journey west from Ohio was not easy. During his first attempt, he was robbed of his supplies and held captive by members of the Pawnee tribe. Upon his release, he returned to Ohio. The following year, 1852, he and his wife Mary crossed the plains successfully. They constructed a house on the S.E. corner of 8th and Exchange Street in Astoria, and then operated a boarding house just west of today's Clatsop County Courthouse.

During the early years, Ross and his wife worked as a team. She cooked for boarders while he attended to basic chores like chopping firewood. It was while performing this menial task that Ross purportedly pushed over the remains of John Jacob Astor's iconic trading post and burned it in his stove. In so doing, he reduced to ashes an internationally significant monument that helped substantiate the United States' claim on the Oregon Country.

Ironically, Ross' less-than-iconic house survives as one of the area's oldest structures. Although now substantially altered, it was once used for the Moose Lodge and the Mormon Church. It currently functions as a wing to Clementine's Bed & Breakfast just above Astoria's commercial district.

Nearly 60 years after the post was destroyed, Astorians sought to correct Ross' folly. A movement developed to reconstruct the fort. Diaries of those associated with early fur trading were brought to the forefront of public consciousness as Astoria prepared for its centennial celebration.

The Centennial Committee, which was comprised of Astoria's most prominent businessmen, considered several venues for the festival. Finalists included one near the ocean. It offered stunning views of the Pacific Ocean and, if selected, would be the first exposition of its kind on the shores of the western continent. Another site was on the edge of Uniontown, Astoria's Finnish district. It presented sweeping views of the Columbia River. In the end, however, it was Shively Park that captured the committee's imagination.

Established in 1899 upon the crest of Astoria's peninsula, the 12-acre Shively Park was near downtown and had land available for exhibition halls. More importantly, the park was chosen for its "unparalleled scenic view" enhanced by the clear-cut flanking its borders. Views to Ft. Clatsop, the mouth of the Columbia and the battlements of Ft. Stevens were vital to reinforce Astoria's prominence in national history.

The site selected to celebrate Astoria's an-

City Park, Astoria, Oregon.

niversary seemed to perfectly reflect the words of Lt. Charles Wilkes, whose expedition visited in 1841. He said, after making catty remarks about the settlement's buildings, "…in point of beauty of situation, few places will vie with Astoria."

After settling on a location, committee members needed to hire an architect to design an exhibit hall, outdoor theater and the reconstruction of Astor's old stockade and blockhouses. Young John E. Wicks, a Swedish-Finn immigrant, was selected. It was natural for Wicks to be a part of Astoria's centennial that celebrated the area's many cultures. Wicks emigrated from Finland in 1899, then made his way to Leadville, Colorado where he worked briefly in a gold mine. There, he earned money for school and learned to speak

English. Wicks later studied architecture at Bethany College in Lindsborg, Kansas. A voracious student, he completed three years worth of coursework in just one year.

In 1904, John Wicks opened his architectural practice in Astoria. A year later, he married Maria Cederberg. She was a maid and cook for Astoria's well-to-do including members of the Capt. Flavel family and candy maker Henry R. Hoefler, whose alcohol-laden "Centennial Chocolates" were the toast of the town.

Wicks quickly captured the admiration of his early clients. His houses were on well-built foundations, constructed "hell for stout." His designs reflected the fashion of the day, frequently recalling elements from the American Colonial period.

Centennial committee members were keenly aware of Wicks' abilities. He finished the construction of Astoria High School just months before winning their contract. The substantial building was the pride of the community. Wicks' gift to meld function with beauty was readily apparent. Because of this, he later won contracts to design virtually every public school in Astoria.

Parenthetically, Wicks' 1911 high school building, now called Towler Hall, will be renovated as the centerpiece of Clatsop Community College's campus. Years of deferred maintenance and just plain butchery are soon to be erased or mollified.

Wicks' approach to Astoria's centennial structures was that of restraint. He was aware of those constructed for Portland's Lewis & Clark Centennial in 1905. Instead of repeating Portland's exotic Spanish and Asian style buildings, his were simpler, more utilitarian. This disparity likely reflects budgetary issues and is not reflective of Wicks' abilities. His design of the Manufacturers' Exhibit Hall is a case in point. The nearly 6,000 sq. ft. wood-framed building was little

Fort Astor, Astoria Centennial, Astoria, Oregon. 1641

more than a double-gabled barn with a decorative, parapet front; a Fish & Fisheries Building was attached to one side. The 1,500 sq. ft. appendage was open to the air and had a canvas roof.

Then there was Wicks' Athenian-inspired outdoor theater. Tucked in the elbow of a hill overlooking Young's Bay, the stadium was carefully planned. No finer, more picturesque theater existed within the lower Columbia region. But, unlike

those in Greece, the seats were made of wood not stone; the forest soon swallowed the auditorium.

When planning the reconstructed trading post, Wicks did his best to evoke Astor's settlement. Dimensions of the 120 by 90-foot complex were lifted from drawings completed by Lt. T. Saumerez, who measured Ft. George in 1818. The new encampment was wrapped within an 8-foot high palisade. Bastions, 18-feet high, were built on either corner. A warehouse, dwelling and shop were constructed within the stockade. Wicks required that all logs remain round, not hewn, and that bark should remain on the timber when possible. Roofing was hand-cut shakes.

The Centennial Committee began the reconstruction of Wicks' trading post on April 12, 1911, precisely 100 years to the day from when the Pacific Fur Company commenced construction of their buildings.

Gabriel Franchere, a Canadian merchant hired by Astor, described the

900 ENTRANCE TO FT ASTOR   ASTORIA ORE.

momentous day in 1811:

"The spring, usually too tardy in this latitude was already far advanced; the foliage was budding, and the earth was clothing itself with verdure, the weather was superb and all nature smiled. We imagined ourselves in the Garden of Eden; the wild forests seemed to us delightful groves and the leaves transformed to brilliant flowers...."

In 1911, snow covered the ground. Access to the park became more challenging. A foot parade, which included a military band from Fort Stevens, coast artillery corps and a battery platoon with two field guns, staggered up the hill from downtown. A ground breaking ceremony was held at the park. The Rev. John Waters offered prayers, school children sang and the coast artillery fired a salute. Construction commenced.

According to the journal of Alexander Ross, a Scottish clerk in the Astor party, there was no end to the difficulty in constructing the original trading post:

"...silent and with heavy hearts we began the toil of the day...in order to secure suitable timbers for this purpose we had to go back some distance, the wood on site being so large and unmanageable, and for want of cattle to haul it, we had to carry it on our shoulders or drag it along the ground, a task of no ordinary difficulty. For this purpose eight men were harnessed and they conveyed in six days all the timber required for a building or store 60 feet long by 26 broad."

Thankfully in 1911, there were legitimate loggers, and if not gas-powered trucks then horse-drawn wagons. Unlike Astor's men, no one involved in the Centennial was crushed by falling trees or had the misfortune to blow their own hand off with a gun. From all known accounts, things went smoothly.

The construction contract was let to Edison & Gamble for $ 2,600. While little is known of Gamble, Jacob Edison built many Astoria houses, constructed numerous public projects and frequently collaborated with Wicks. Edison completed construction of the new trading post in two months. Then, he quickly departed and commenced construction of a new hospital at the quarantine station in Megler, Washington. Known as the Columbia River's "Ellis Island," it is now one of the most underrated, little known

landmarks and museums in our area.

Arthur L. Peck was hired to lay out the city park for the Centennial. Peck was the founder of the Landscape Architecture School at Oregon Agricultural College, now Oregon State University. He founded the program in 1908 and is credited with introducing the western United States to formal training in landscape architecture. Furthermore, he was responsible for all landscape planning on the OSU campus.

Peck used now-familiar plantings including European varieties of Purple Beech, White Birch and Mountain Ash. Rather than plant tree rows, Peck laid out vegetation according to naturalistic curves. Trees were placed for their romantic appeal, framing views and emphasizing the undulating landscape.

The park plan was like an oval, cut in half across its width. Entry to the park was in the lower half. There, visitors were immediately struck by the reconstruction of Astor's trading post. A forest was maintained and replanted behind it as a backdrop to the historical set piece. Both intellectual and emotional associations to Astoria's past became forefront in the mind of the observer. After passing through the "forest primeval," visitors were rewarded by broad vistas, shaped by ornamental plantings. Here, the educational component was found. Exhibition halls, an Indian encampment and the outdoor theater all played off the historically significant sites within view of the park.

It was a magnificent setting. The park and its structures served the community well. However, when the celebration ended, the park fell silent.

976 LOOKING UP YOUNGS RIVER FROM CENTRAL PARK. ASTORIA ORE.

Minor events were held there, but essentially the structures were left to rot and the landscape was not adequately maintained.

In 1917, the reconstructed trading post was donated to local Boy Scout troops for use as their headquarters. The boys carried out drills, held camp meetings and evening reveries. It must have been every boy's dream come true. But the fun ended shortly. In 1920, it was determined that the structure was unsafe and in a rapid state of decay. The City of Astoria tore down "Fort Astor."

Years later, the Clatsop County Historical Society determined that what our community really lacked was a reconstruction of Astor's trading post. It turned to John Wicks for help. He dusted off his 1911 drawings and proposed a modest memorial. In 1956, a partial reconstruction was built on 15th and Exchange Street—site of the original 1811 trading post. Wolmanized logs, left over from the reconstruction of Ft. Clatsop, were used to construct a bastion.

Local signmaker Arvid Wuonola provided a bit of context by painting a mural on the wall behind the monument. Since then, the mural has been reinterpreted several times, but never more beautifully than by Roger McKay and Sally Lackaff in 2002. The false perspective is perfect. Local Chinookan people are portrayed with dignity, too.

As Astoria prepares to celebrate its bicentennial in 2011, organizers will have one less thing to worry about. Wick's reconstruction remains in good condition. And unlike its predecessors, the bastion is in no danger of being pushed over or chopped into pieces for firewood.

SESQUICENTENNIAL CELEBRATION
August 1961

One hundred and fifty years is a respectable anniversary, but sesquicentennials never seem to get the same billing as full-century commemorations. Such was the case in Astoria in 1961. The city had truly outdone itself with the Centennial Celebration of 1911, and as another half-century elapsed, sesquicentennial planners looked to combine the event with the historic Regatta Festival.

April of 1961 witnessed the official sesquicentennial commemoration. There to mark the occasion were members of the Astor family: Lord John Jacob Astor V, The First Baron Astor of Hever and Lady Violet Astor, Hon. Gavin and Lady Irene Astor, and their teenage son John Jacob Astor VIII. Mayor Harry Steinbock and other dignitaries escorted the Astors through Astoria

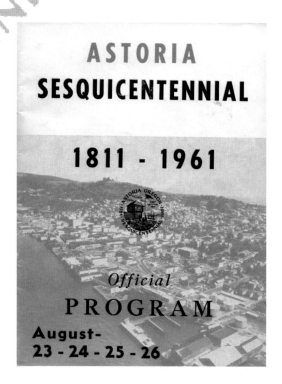

and Seaside. One of their stops was at the Astoria Column, where Lord Astor dedicated a monument to the Chinook Indians, a replica of Chief Comcomly's burial canoe.

The Regatta-Sesquicentennial got underway on Thursday, August 24. The pageantry began when Mayor Steinbock crowed Sally Romppanen, a blue-eyed, blonde-haired Astoria High School senior Sesquicentennial Queen. That evening premiered a John B. Rogers production entitled "Sesqui – A – Storia," a 16-part play depicting the area's history. The cast of this theatrical epic included scores of Astorians who, despite a notable lack of thespian talent, performed with great zest.

On Friday, the buildup continued as Clair Ann Hellmann of Knappa was crowned Regatta Queen amid much fanfare. The evening featured

Astoria Mayor Harry Steinbock greets Lord and Lady Astor as they arrive to take part in the sesquicentennial celebration in the spring of 1961.

on festooned in flotsam, to The Sons & Daughters of Norway's log cabin peopled with pioneers and Native Americans. Also in the procession were lock-stepping drill teams, high-stepping majorettes, and the Astoria Clowns. In addition to the customary drum corps and marching bands the musical assortment included Iola's Accordion Band, Portland's Scottish Bag Pipes, and Nomadettes Glockenspiel Band. The newspaper declared it to be a "tuneful spectacle."

In addition to being Astoria's birthday, the weekend also featured the traditional Regatta festivities. Some 2,000 boats took to the water—many in search of salmon—while at the East Mooring Basin the hydro races were in full swing.

Like the Centennial Celebration a half-century before, Astoria's Sesquicentennial had a lasting

legacy. There was the aforementioned Chief Comcomly replica burial canoe monument to the Chinook Indians located near the foot of the Astoria Column. Additionally, generous donations by the Astor family and other groups funded the construction of a new public library that opened in 1967. Astoria's 150th birthday party had indeed been a success, and despite being a lowly sesquicentennial, commemorated the city's history and significance admirably.

an International Smorgasbord and enough revelry that the *Daily Astorian* predicted: "If all goes well, Monday should be the worst Monday-after in Astoria history."

Saturday, August 26 was the big day. An estimated 12,000 people turned out for the gala parade that featured 110 entries. The floats ranged from Netarts' Beachcombers' Float, a station wag-

Astoria's Story 1811-2011

This year marks the 200th anniversary of the founding of Astoria, Oregon, the oldest American settlement west of the Rocky Mountains. Over the next 100 pages join the Clatsop County Historical Society as it looks back on Astoria's first two centuries in both words and images in...

An Adventure in History...

Historical Astoria:
An Overview

by Carlos A. Schwantes
St. Louis Mercantile Library
Professor of the American West

In seeking to account for the growth and development of historical Astoria, I am inclined to cite the mantra so often repeated by real estate agents: "location, location, location." Few other cities in Oregon, or even in the United States, can claim a more favorable natural setting.

Back in the early 1800s, when waterways constituted the Interstate highways of the era, Mother Nature favored Astoria with easy access to two of the world's greatest water highways: the Columbia River and the Pacific Ocean. The wide Columbia flowed past Astoria's front doorstep and linked the settlement to the Pacific Ocean only a few miles west, as well as to the vast hinterland drained by the river to the east. Thus Astoria formed a logical connection between East and West, a commercial link between the distant and often exotic lands lapped by the Pacific Ocean and the natural resource-rich forests, fields, and mines of the Pacific Northwest.

Even before there was an American settlement named Astoria, the site was already rich in history. In the fall of 1805 Lewis and Clark had established their Pacific Coast base nearby, at what is now the site of Fort Clatsop; in 1811, the fur merchant John Jacob Astor had built his West Coast base of Astoria; and even earlier, in the 1790s, the mariners Robert Gray and James Cook had introduced the region and its natural resources, to the EuroAmerican world. Before the area's "discovery" by the outside world, Native Americans of the lower Columbia enjoyed such an abundance

of nature's food resources that they had plenty of time left over to develop an elaborate material culture.

Astoria itself thrived for a time as a result of the thick stands of timber that crowded the river's bank. To one observer, the settlement's sawmills were processing timber at a furious pace lest the forest grow faster than the wood could be processed and crowd the town back into the river. In addition, migratory salmon and other marine edibles once thrived in the Columbia and other local waters, which collectively provided the basis for one of the greatest concentration of canneries in the lower forty-eight states. At one time in the 1880s and 1890s, the Astoria area could boast of

no fewer than twenty-five canneries. Production of canned salmon peaked in the late 1800s, and eventually the industry relocated from the Columbia River to the pristine waters of Puget Sound and later Alaska.

Astoria's prosperity rested on a varied population of natives and immigrants whose presence added to the city's colorful history. The area's fishermen were for the most part Scandinavians and Finns who, to make ends meet, logged or farmed nearby lands in the slow season. Many of Astoria's cannery workers were Chinese. That was because catching fish was far more desirable work than processing them. Canning initially was a slow, messy, and smelly craft, with each of the millions of cans requiring careful soldering by hand. A revolutionary machine introduced in 1905 and called the Iron Chink (with unselfconscious racism) dramatically thinned the ranks of Astoria's cannery workers by doing the work of fifty men. It was one of many technological changes that would impact the fortunes of Astoria over the years. Equally challenging to the community were the boom-and-bust cycles that defined so many of its basic industries.

For many years, Astoria residents witnessed a daily parade of steamboats, both great and small, running up and down the Columbia River, some carrying travelers on business and also tourists enjoying the sights between Portland and vaca-

tion resorts on the Oregon coast, all in addition to many tons of freight. Many steamboats were quite elegant, and one local favorite was the sternwheeler *Bailey Gatzert*, which was featured on a United States postage stamp in 1996. In addition, steamships designed for ocean travel carried cargoes of commodities from Astoria and the Pacific Northwest to ports as distant as Ireland and Australia.

However, once again changes in technology forced Astoria to adjust. First came the railroads and then the highways and automobiles, which together diminished and then destroyed steamboat traffic along the Columbia River. Yet, the automobile also opened Astoria and the Oregon Coast to an even greater influx of tourists, and today's Highway 101, a popular route stretching from southern California to northwestern Washington, crosses the Columbia on the majestic Astoria-Megler bridge, the last one on the river. Among the area's many attractions is Astoria's charming 1920s-era downtown.

Thinking about distant Astoria from my desk in St. Louis is really not such a strange pastime, given that the currents of history once linked the destinies of the two communities. Members of the Lewis and Clark expedition, for example, spent the winter of 1803-04 encamped along the Mississippi River near St. Louis, while their co-captain, Meriwether Lewis, learned all he could about the way west from the explorers and fur merchants who made their homes in the city. Later when John Jacob Astor wanted to establish a base for his fur trade near the mouth of the Columbia River (and the main reason Astoria will celebrate its

bicentennial in 2011), he chose a St. Louis merchant, Wilson Price Hunt, to head an overland expedition to the site of his future Fort Astoria.

Until the United States acquired California from Mexico and gained clear title to Puget Sound during the mid 1840s, the nation's only certain gateway to the Pacific was the Columbia River, with the little settlement of Astoria occupying a position of strategic importance. For a time during the 1840s, Astoria could boast of the only United States Post Office located west of Missouri. One of the biggest boosters on Capitol Hill of better transportation between the United States and its outpost at the mouth of the Columbia River was Thomas Hart Benton, Missouri's first federal Senator. It is not too much to argue that St. Louis and Astoria were once the twin gateways between which lay the American West waiting to be explored and defined cartographically by three generations of adventurers, mapmakers, artists, soldiers, and entrepreneurs of various types, and transformed into countless homes for the families of farmers, fishermen, loggers, miners, laborers, craftsmen, merchants, preachers, teachers, and anyone else inclined to face the challenges of making a living in challenging but rewarding new land. The result, as they say, is history.

The First Peoples

No one can say with certainty when *the First Peoples* arrived on the lower Columbia River. Archeological evidence suggests that it was three or four thousand years ago, perhaps longer. In all those centuries the people fished and traded, occasionally warred and generally prospered.

Eventually, the four groups that would come to be known collectively as Chinooks—the Clatsops, Kathlamets, Wahkiakums, and Shoalwater Chinook—established territories. The Clatsops lived on the Columbia's south shore, from Tongue Point west to the Pacific Ocean and south to Tillamook Head; the Kathlamets dwelt around Cathlamet Bay on the Columbia's south shore above Tongue Point; the Wahkiakums resided from Deep River east to Oak Point; and the Shoalwater Chinook, or Chinook proper, lived on the river's north bank between Grays Bay and the Pacific Ocean, and north around portions of Willapa Bay.

Artwork by Roger McKay

Strategically located between inland tribes and those along the Pacific Coast, the Chinooks occupied the crossroads of a major trade network. They capitalized on this location and came to enjoy wealth unknown to most North American Indians. The Chinook economy included trade in arrowheads, baskets, beads, berries, canoes, furs, leather, shells, salmon, slaves, and whale oil and blubber. Of all the Native Americans trafficking goods throughout the Northwest, the Chinooks were perhaps the most astute bargain makers and among them trading became well-honed art. Later contact with white traders only increased the Chinooks' wealth and business acumen.

The Chinooks' preoccupation with trade was made possible by the natural abundance of their surroundings. They spent most of the year in villages along the Columbia River, fishing, feasting, and trading. The Big River provided a bountiful harvest of steelhead, salmon, smelt, sturgeon, and waterfowl. From the seashore and bays came a multitude of shellfish, and just inland, wild cranberries. As fall approached, most Chinooks would relocate to villages in the hills away from the coast where they would winter. With the arrival of spring they would once again migrate back to their fishing grounds along the Columbia as part of this rhythmic natural cycle.

What the waters did not provide, the forest did. Foodstuffs like salal and salmon berries, edible roots, and large game were plentiful most years. From the forests, too, came western red cedar, the substance from which they crafted most of their material goods. From single cedar logs, Native woodworkers fashioned dugout canoes, many over 50 feet in length, which provided the Chinooks with their primary means of long-distance trans-

portation and helped facilitate their intricate trade networks. From the cedars' bark, branches, and roots, skilled weavers fashioned watertight robes, hats, baskets, and fishing nets.

"Tribes" were of little importance to the Chinooks. Instead, their fundamental socio-political unit was the village. Here, extended families dwelt in cavernous cedar-plank longhouses neatly situated in rows not far from the water's edge. Larger Chinook villages, like Qwatsamts near present-day Megler, Washington, were known to contain some 30 longhouses.

Within these villages the Chinooks had a stratified social structure where heredity and wealth determined rank. The two fundamental classes were freemen and slaves, though among

freemen there were nuanced gradients in status. The Chinooks had no chiefs, as commonly pictured in popular culture, but high-ranking males often assumed leadership roles, usually in hereditary succession. Headmen were chosen by the consensus of the village dwellers, and if they proved unworthy leaders would be replaced in this loosely democratic system. Women sometimes held positions of power as well with the elders active in village councils, but generally their social standing was secondary to that of men.

Slavery was a common practice among Northwest Coast Indians, including the Chinooks. The slaves were either purchased or taken as spoils of victory in battles between warring villages. The Chinooks compelled their slaves to do the most wearisome tasks like carrying water, gathering wood, and paddling their master's canoe. Slaves were also used as a means of barter and were even given as gifts. Any free Chinook could own slaves but oftentimes only the wealthy were able to afford them. According to author Rick Rubin, 10 to 25-percent of the population of a Chinookan village was held in bondage.

A striking feature among the Chinookan people, and one that separated free persons from slaves, was the artificial flattening of the forehead. The deformation of the skull began at birth when the mother tied her newborn onto a cradleboard and laced a fur-padded plank over the infant's head. As the child grew its brow became elongated, which in Chinook culture was an unequivocal sign of both beauty and freedom.

In the early 1780s, life as the Clatsops, Kathlamets, Wahkiakums, and Shoalwater Chinook had known it was jarred by disease. It was smallpox, and to Native Americans that had no immunity to the scourge, it was lethal. The pestilence spread from village to village wiping out entire families. As contact with Euro-American traders increased in the decades to follow, so too did the occurrence of disease: tuberculosis, scarlet fever, measles, influenza. In some instances, so many people were infected by "the fever and ague" that the dead lay where they fell, the survivors unable to attend to all of the corpses.

Two of the leading Chinookan nobles to emerge during these early years of contact with Euro-Americans and their diseases were the Clatsop Cobaway and Comcomly, a Shoalwater Chinook. As their villages' headmen they greeted incoming trading ships, which put them in an advantageous position when it came time to barter. Their wealth and status grew. To cement trading connections with the newly founded settlement of Astoria, both Cobaway and Comcomly exercised the long-established Chinook custom of marrying their daughters to prominent traders, Americans and British alike.

Despite the Chinooks' increasing material wealth, the great die-off continued through the early decades of the 1800s. Like the vast majority of their people, Cobaway succumbed to disease in 1824, followed six years later by Comcomly. By the 1840s, the Chinook population was a mere fraction of what it had been only a generation earlier. With their culture unraveling, some survivors attempted to cope with the incomprehensible tragedy through alcohol, and soon alcoholism was sweeping the Native Americans away as well.

White settlers, whose sympathies for the native population varied by the individual, began staking claims to village sites and fishing grounds. The government actively encouraged the settlement and private ownership of the land, a notion that Native Americans could scarcely understand. Talk began to circulate among the settlers of moving the remaining Chinooks onto inland reservations. In 1850, the U.S. Congress created the Office of Superintendent of Indian Affairs of Oregon, and the following year one of its representatives, Anson Dart, met with the Chinook people at Tansey Point.

Dart's initial objective at the Tansey Point treaty council was to get the various bands of Chinooks to agree to relocate to reservations east of the Cascade Mountains where they would be out of the way of white settlers. This idea the attendees patently rejected. Instead, they agreed to cede their lands for trivial cash payments payable over 10 years. The Clatsops, the first group Dart dealt with, demanded a tiny reservation at Point Adams to which the Indian agent conceded. Over a week's time Dart executed 13 treaties, but when they reached Washington D.C. Congress shelved them and they were never ratified. Government payment for the lands would never arrive, but more land-hungry settlers did.

One of the Clatsops likely in attendance at Tansey Point in 1851, was a woman in her thirties named Tsin-is-tum. She came from noble bloodlines, as did her Nehalem husband who died less than a decade after the treaty convention. Tsin-is-tum married again, this time to settler Michel Martineau. It was then that Tsin-is-tum became Jennie Michel. By 1900, the self-proclaimed centurion had become one of Seaside's leading attractions, selling her hand-woven baskets to summer visitors and posing for innumerable photographs, so many in fact, that a correspondent from the *Oregonian* thought she may have been the most photographed person in the entire state.

Jennie Michel's passing in 1905 made headlines in newspapers across the region. She was mourned as "the last of the Clatsops," and her obituary read like a eulogy for an entire people. Tsin-is-tum, Jennie Michel, had lived through the greatest period of anguish and acculturation that her people would

Jennie Michel

know, but the story of the lower Columbia's First Peoples did not end with her. Descendants of the Clatsops, Kathlamets, Wahkiakums, and Shoalwater Chinook still reside in Astoria and elsewhere. Today they are working to regain their ancestral traditions and history as well as formal recognition from the federal government.

Read More...

An authoritative history of the lower Columbia's First Peoples has never been written by one of their own. Scholars have done much to tell their story and numerous books address the topic. One of the finest is Naked Against the Rain: The People of the Lower Columbia River, 1770-1830, penned by Portland free-lance writer Rick Rubin (Far Shore Press, 1999).

Columbia's River

In March of 1778, the two ships of Captain James Cook's third great voyage of discovery cast their anchors in the sheltered waters of Nootka Sound, on the west coast of Vancouver Island. Now in the second year of their expedition, the British sailors and officers stood in tattered uniforms as canoes full of Indians cloaked in long, lustrous fur robes came alongside the ships. To fend off the chill air, the ships' crews bartered with the Natives for the warm capes. This unremarkable act of self-preservation became remarkable when the ships, *Discovery* and *Resolution,* reached Canton that December, and the sailors found the Chinese willing to pay hefty sums in silver coin for the sea otter furs.

When Cook's ships returned to England in 1780, news of this new commercial opportunity spread. By the end of the decade, the Pacific fur trade was in full swing. Trading ships coasted the Pacific shoreline, looking for inlets and outlets where they found Native Americans willing to trade furs for metal knickknacks, heavy cloth, beads, and even muskets. Once enough pelts were collected, the vessels crossed the ocean to China where the furs were exchanged for stores of Asiatic goods like tea, spices, silk, and porcelain, which in turn were sold in western markets for extraordinary profits.

The Russians, Spanish, and British had an early lead in the maritime fur trade, but by 1787 Americans had entered the field. In that year, the *Columbia Rediviva,* under the command of Captain John Kendrick, and her tender, *Lady Washington*, skippered by Captain Robert Gray, sailed from Boston.

Artwork Courtesy of Oregon State Capitol, Legislative Administration Committee

Nearly a year was spent trading along the coasts of what became Oregon, Washington, and British Columbia before the captains switched ships and Gray piloted the *Columbia* to Canton. When Gray and the *Columbia* arrived back in Boston in August of 1790, they were celebrated as the first Americans to have circumnavigated the globe.

Though the *Columbia Rediviva's* first fur trading voyage had been a financial disappointment, on October 2, 1790 she set sail once again for the Pacific Ocean with Captain Gray at her helm. *Columbia's* crew began collecting furs along the Northwest Coast in the summer of 1791 and spent the winter in Clayoquot Sound, an inlet just north of Nootka Sound. The following spring, Gray and his small band of sailors headed south.

On April 28, 1792, while off the northern Washington Coast, the *Columbia* was hailed by the *Discovery* and *Chatham,* British ships under the

command of Captain George Vancouver and Lieutenant William Broughton, respectively. The captains exchanged information on their recent discoveries and soon parted ways. Nine days later, Gray steered the *Columbia* into a bay he named Bullfinch Harbor, in honor of Charles Bullfinch, one of the Boston merchants backing the voyage. After a couple days of trading, the *Columbia* left the bay that cartographers later called Grays Harbor, sailing south once again.

Early on the morning of May 11, 1792, Gray spotted another promising inlet. The log of the *Columbia Rediviva* recounts: "At eight, A.M., being a little to the windward of the entrance of the Harbor, bore away, and run in east-north-east between the breakers, having from five to seven fathoms of water. When we were over the bar, we found this to be a large river of fresh water, up which we steered." Gray anchored his ship off the north shore near an Indian village and commenced trading. Furs and salmon were plentiful and, as the Yankee noted, "bought cheap." It was not until May 19th that Gray decided to name this waterway "*Columbia's River.*"

Had he not been the first Euro-American to enter the great river, Gray would probably be a mere footnote in maritime history. That he was born in Rhode Island in the year 1755 of old New England stock is the only indisputable information of his early life. His appearance, too, is a matter of conjecture, as the only attributable portraits of him were created after his death. The logbooks from Gray's two voyages to the Pacific provide the

only clues to the bearing of the celebrated navigator. After he returned to Boston in July of 1793, he married, went back to sea, and essentially slips from the historical record. Even the date and location of his passing remain unclear.

Much ink has been spilt celebrating Gray's providential "discovery" of the Columbia River, the entrance to which had been sighted by numerous mariners. As early as the 1600s, Spanish explorers had recorded what appeared to be a great river near 46-degrees north latitude. Spaniard Bruno de Heceta first charted the river's entrance in 1775, naming the stream Rio San Roque. Thirteen years later, British Lieutenant John Meares spied what he took to be the fabled river but, being rebuffed by a wall of breakers at its entrance, he named the promontory at its northern shore Cape Disappointment. Even Captain George Vancouver had passed by the broad inlet in April of 1792, noting in his log that it was not "worthy of more attention."

Vancouver's opinion changed considerably, however, when he learned that Captain Gray had indeed entered and named Columbia's River. Vancouver sent Lieutenant Broughton into the river

to conduct a survey. Following a crude chart drawn by Gray, Broughton guided the *Chatham* across the bar on October 21, 1792, where he found to his surprise the British brig *Jenny*, under Captain James Baker, trading with local Indians.

The nomenclature

of the lower Columbia owes much to Broughton. He named the bay where the *Jenny* was anchored Baker's Bay, and just upstream labeled the river entering from the south Young's River, after his uncle Sir George Young. Broughton and a small party left the *Chatham* in what he called Gray's Bay and continued upriver in longboats. Over the following week he affixed names to every prominent landmark, including Puget Island (for Lt. Peter Puget of the *Discovery*), Mt. Hood (for Sir Samuel Hood of the British Admiralty), and Point Vancouver (for the captain of *Discovery*).

The Columbia River was the last great discovery made by Euro-American traders and explorers along the Northwest Coast. The urge to trade may have carried Captain Gray into this waterway, but in so doing he established the United States' first legitimate claim over European powers to the Columbia River Basin.

READ MORE...

Among the most insightful histories of the maritime fur trade was one written by John Scofield, a descendant of Captain John Kendrick. His book, Hail, Columbia: Robert Gray, John Kendrick and the Pacific Fur Trade, *was published by the Oregon Historical Society Press in 1993.*

THE CORPS of Discovery

"Ocian in view! O! the joy" scribbled Captain William Clark in his leather-bound field notes on the wet and blustery afternoon of November 7, 1805. Captain Clark, his co-commander Meriwether Lewis, and the bedraggled members of their Corps of Discovery had trekked over four thousand miles to reach this point, the fulfillment of their western exploration.

Some 18 months earlier, the 31 members of the Corps of Discovery had started up the Missouri River at the behest of President Thomas Jefferson to examine the unmapped western half of the continent. Jefferson was keenly interested in this unexplored country, seeing in its broad expanses unlimited potential for the young nation. He instructed Lewis and Clark to chart with "great pains & accuracy" the most direct water route to the Western Ocean, and along the way document its geography, inhabitants, and economic opportunities.

Now, from their encampment near Pillar Rock the expedition members could see white-capped waves where the Columbia River disappeared into the Pacific Ocean. Hampered by a savage storm and ripping tides, the expedition made little head-

way, not rounding Point Ellice as a group until November 15. Along a sandy beach near present-day McGowan, Washington, the Corps set up Station Camp, which would be their home for the next 10 days.

From Station Camp, both captains took turns reconnoitering Cape Disappointment and the south Long Beach Peninsula hoping to find an outpost of white traders rumored to reside there. No trading post was located, but to mark the occasion, Clark drew his knife and scribed on a handy tree "By Land from the U. States in 1804 & 1805."

Where to spend the fast-approaching winter soon became an issue. On November 24, a democratic vote was held—the first of its kind in the Pacific Northwest—where all registered

their opinion, including the Shoshone woman, Sacagawea, and Captain Clark's slave, York. With only one dissenting vote, the decision to explore the possibilities of the south shore of the Columbia River won. After a brief but tumultuous reconnaissance, a suitable site for winter quarters was found along the Netul River, a short distance upstream from Youngs Bay.

The Corps began construction of a fort December 7, 1805. The 50-foot square stockade, which they named Fort Clatsop, was completed five days after Christmas. A salt-making station was established at modern-day Seaside where crews set to work boiling sea water to collect the precious preservative.

Fort life quickly settled into a cheerless routine. The men quelled their boredom with busy-work, crafting hundreds of pairs of moccasins and other necessities for the return trip. Captain Lewis spent the winter describing the flora and fauna around Fort Clatsop, while Captain Clark focused on compiling a map of their westward journey. It was a damp and disagreeable time for the expedition.

While at Fort Clatsop, Lewis and Clark showed little hospitality toward their Native neighbors. According to historian James Rhonda, the chilly relations were due to the fact that the captains neither liked nor trusted the coastal Indians. The Corps had had some unfavorable encounters with some of the Chinookan people while at Station Camp and found their hard bargaining tactics—honed by years of bartering with maritime fur traders—to be unreasonable. The Indians were kept at arm's length with only a select few permitted to enter the fort.

After three and a half dreary months at Fort Clatsop, the Corps of Discovery headed upriver on March 23, 1806, returning safely to St. Louis that September. They had been gone for two years and five months. Besides returning with a wealth of observations regarding natural science, the Corps had mapped the unknown void between the Missouri River and the Pacific Ocean. Though they did not find a direct water route linking the continent, the Lewis and Clark expedition had made the West something the American mind could better comprehend.

Astorians have always had an interest in Fort Clatsop. Some of the original Astorians, in fact,

Photos Courtesy of the National Park Service

were the first tourists to visit the site in 1811. Since then it has been a regular point of interest for sightseers. In the 1850s, the last rotting remains of Lewis and Clark's winter quarters could still be seen, though land clearing activities soon made the fort's footprint indistinguishable. Efforts were made to determine the precise location of the fort, and in 1901 the Oregon Historical Society purchased the site.

In 1955, a replica of Fort Clatsop was built on what is likely the exact spot Captain Lewis had chosen 150 years earlier. Three years later, Congress established the site, now encompassing 125 acres, as a national memorial. Amid the Corps of Discovery's bicentennial, in 2004 the memorial was re-designated the Lewis and Clark National Historical Park. Added to Fort Clatsop were other key Lewis and Clark locations in both Oregon and Washington, including Dismal Nitch, the Salt Works, and Station Camp. In 2005, the fort was destroyed by fire. Through a community-wide effort crews erected a more accurate replica, which they finished just in time for the bicentennial activities.

Read More…

History professors always urge their students to "go to the source," and few primary documents are as engaging as the journals of the Lewis and Clark Expedition. In this field the preeminent compendium is The Definitive Journals of Lewis & Clark: Down the Columbia to Fort Clatsop, insightfully edited by Gary Moulton (Lincoln: University of Nebraska Press, 1990).

Astoria as it appeared in 1813.

THE Founding OF ASTORIA

The morning of Friday, April 12, 1811, was clear and pleasant. On that memorable day, a party of Pacific Fur Company employees began clearing a site for a trading post on a forested hill above the south shore of the Columbia River some 12 miles from the Pacific Ocean. Within a week they began squaring timbers for a storehouse and turning soil for a garden. "We make but little progress in clearing," noted one of the clerks, "the place being so full of half decayed trunks, large fallen timber & thick brush." On April 21, the builders named their fledgling establishment Astoria.

In 1811, the western frontier of American settlement extended only to the Mississippi Valley. The vast and largely unexplored portion of North America beyond the Mississippi was an international battleground for European powers vying to expand their empires. From the north, Russian settlements were spreading southward while the British Empire had emissaries coursing though Canada and pushing toward the Pacific. From the south came the Spanish, whose imperial outposts had been creeping northward for centuries. In the middle of this sat Astoria, the lone American colony in this contested region.

The planner, financier, and now namesake of this westernmost outpost was John Jacob Astor. A native of Germany, Astor had become involved in the fur trade almost as soon as he landed in America in 1784. With limitless ambition, the young immigrant climbed to the top of the mercantile world of New York, propelled largely by the shipment of furs and pelts to Europe. By the early 1800s, Astor was reaping huge profits from his newly opened fur trade with China, but a roundtrip voyage from New York to Canton was excruciatingly slow.

By 1808, Astor had a more direct route to Asia in mind. He envisioned a string of fur trading posts up the Missouri River, over the Rocky Mountains, and along the Columbia River with direct access to Chinese markets. He would start with a fur emporium at the mouth of the Columbia, which would be his Pacific Coast headquarters. With this strategic foothold, Astor believed, he could monopolize the fur trade across this broad expanse of continent.

To undertake such a grand venture, Astor sought a partnership with his old Canadian competitor, the North West Fur Company, and the support of the United States government. Eliciting aid from these two entities proved a ticklish matter, as the new relationship between the United States and Great Britain following the War for Independence was still somewhat tempestuous. After showing some initial interest, the Nor'westers politely declined. In the meantime, Astor spread word of his proposal among Washington's elite, including President Thomas Jefferson, in carefully worded and somewhat vague missives. Jefferson, for his part, responded in equally vague terms, assuring "every reasonable patronage and facility in the power of the Executive will be afford."

In March of 1810, Astor organized the Pacific Fur Company, pledging $400,000 and controlling one-half of the shares. Astor sought out the most able men to bring his plan to fruition, and to ensure their loyalty and motivation made a number of them minor partners. Former Nor'westers Alexander McKay and Duncan McDougall, with brothers David and Robert Stuart, were hired to lead a ma-

rine expedition around Cape Horn and establish the trading post while an American, Wilson Price Hunt, agreed to lead an overland party with Canadian Donald McKenzie as his second in command. Joining the overland expedition would be partners Ramsay Crooks, Robert McClellan, and Joseph Miller.

Astor purchased a sturdy ship named *Tonquin* and put at her helm Jonathan Thorn, a capable United States navy lieutenant on official leave. On September 6, 1810, the *Tonquin*, loaded with over $50,000 worth of supplies and trade goods set sail from New York harbor. Thorn's inflexible and peevish character soon became problematic and served to heighten tensions throughout the voyage. After touching in Hawaii to pick up laborers, the *Tonquin* hove near the Columbia River bar in March 1811. Thorn ordered eight men out in a whaleboat to sound for a passable channel across the bar, but none returned. A few days later, on March 25, the weather moderated and the *Tonquin* entered the Columbia.

From the *Tonquin's* anchorage in Bakers Bay, the fur traders occupied several weeks looking for the proper place to locate Astor's outpost. A rolling, timber-covered hill on the Columbia's southern shore was selected as the location for the enterprise. The site did not wholly satisfy the partners, but Captain Thorn had orders from Astor to continue his trading mis-

sion up the coast and had grown anxious to leave. With only a storehouse and shed completed at Astoria, the *Tonquin* caught a favorable wind and sailed from the Columbia on the fifth of June.

Meanwhile, Wilson Price Hunt's overland party had left Montreal in the summer of 1810, picking up American and Canadian trappers as they headed toward St. Louis. The expedition, consisting of nearly 50 men, had planned to follow the route pioneered by Lewis and Clark, but rumors of hostile Indians on the upper reaches of the Missouri River convinced Hunt to leave the established route. The results were disastrous. After losing their way, the group splintered and suffered numerous privations and a several deaths before reaching the Snake River. The first of the overland party arrived in Astoria in January of 1812, but Hunt and his detachment did not appear until the end of February.

On May 5, 1812, Astor's ship *Beaver* arrived at the outpost carrying a third contingent of

Astorians. The ship also brought news confirming a rumor that the Astorians had heard concerning the destruction of the *Tonquin*. They discovered that after leaving the Columbia, the *Tonquin* sailed north trading along the coast as ordered. Off Vancouver Island, Captain Thorn outraged an Indian headman during a trade dispute by rubbing a pelt in his

"In the garden of Eden, the Founding of Astoria, April 1811," watercolor, by Mark Myers.

face. This act provoked the Indians to overrun the ship the following morning. One sailor survived, so the Astorians were told, and slipped below decks to ignite the ship's powder store, obliterating the *Tonquin* and all onboard.

Despite the tragedy, Astor's plan was taking shape. Upriver posts were established, first with Fort Okanogan and then Fort Spokane. The *Beaver* had brought a fresh supply of trade goods and Astor's men were finding the country rich in furs. But as the Astorians' prospects began to look brighter, international affairs intervened.

On January 15, 1813, Donald McKenzie reached Astoria with word from the interior that the United States was at war with Great Britain. He also reported that the British ship *Isaac Todd*

was en route to the Columbia to capture Astoria. That October, a flotilla of canoes carrying 75 employees of the North West Company landed at Astoria to await the arrival of the *Isaac Todd*. Under duress, Duncan McDougall decided to sell the post and its stockpile of furs to the Nor'Westers for a fraction of its actual value.

It was not the *Isaac Todd*, but the faster sloop-of-war *Racoon* that entered the Columbia to capture the Pacific Fur Company's headquarters. Determined to carry out his orders despite the sale of Astoria two months prior, Captain William Black of the *Racoon*, went ashore and oversaw its formal surrender on December 12, 1813. The Union Jack was hoisted and Astoria became a wartime prize of Great Britain.

Captain Black left Astoria in the hands of the North West Company, who renamed it Fort George. The War of 1812 formally ended on

Christmas Eve 1814, when the Treaty of Ghent was signed. Included in this treaty was a provision that all lands captured during the conflict be returned to the country with previous title. No one knew what to do with Astoria—Astor claimed Captain Black had captured his outpost, while the Nor'Westers held that they had legally purchased it before Black's arrival. With his Columbia River monopoly ruined, Astor chose to give up on his ambitious western plan, and with it the American presence at Astoria.

When the *Isaac Todd* finally arrived at Fort George in April of 1814, none of its cargo excited more interest than a blonde-haired, blue-eyed English barmaid named Jane Barnes. The first Euro-American woman in Astoria—and indeed the first in the entire Pacific Northwest—Jane was the concubine of Donald McTavish, a North West Company official. Upon McTavish's drowning, Jane was proposed to by Cassakas, a son of the Chinook tribal leader Comcomly. He offered her 100 sea otter skins, a life of leisure, and superiority over his other wives. Unfortunately, the nature of her refusal went unrecorded. Jane shipped out of Fort George in the late summer or fall on a ship bound for Canton, but her exploits in Astoria have remained a popular topic of conversation in local classrooms and barrooms for nearly two centuries.

In 1818, a joint occupancy treaty was signed, giving both the United States and Great Britain equal claims to the Pacific Northwest. Three years later the Hudson's Bay Company (HBC) absorbed the North West Company, and later under factor George Simpson moved their headquarters some ninety miles upriver where they established Fort Vancouver. The Columbia River, HBC governors reasoned, might well become the international boundary between the United States and British

Canada, and forthrightly centered their energies on the north shore. In the process, the HBC essentially abandoned Fort George, seldom stationing more than a handful of employees there. The soggy coastal climate began to wear away at Astoria's fortifications, and by the 1830s little remained except for a few log cabins.

But even as the real Astoria was deteriorating, a symbolic Astoria was flourishing. In 1834, an aging John Jacob Astor approached Washington Irving, then America's most celebrated author, to write the story of the venture. Astor hoped the book would secure his place in history as a true patriot and visionary, and to that end offered Irving a handsome stipend. In the fall of 1836, *Astoria, or Anecdotes of an Enterprise Beyond the Rocky Mountains*, was published and became an instant success, with multiple editions printed in English, German, and French. Irving's book made Astoria an icon of the American West. The monograph ended with a prophetic statement, which declared that Astoria might "become the watchword in a

contest for dominion on the shores of the Pacific."

In 1844, James K. Polk was elected president of the United States on an expansionist platform calling, in part, to re-occupy Oregon. Speeches on the floor of Congress trumpeted the importance of the American settlement at Astoria as sure proof of the nation's claim to the region. One such speech came from the fiery Missouri Senator Thomas Hart Benton, who declared before the Senate in May of 1846 that Astoria was the "cornerstone" of America's "unquestionable" right over the British to the valley of the Columbia. The very name Astoria, he insisted, is "in itself the badge of American title." Although Astoria's importance to the Pacific fur trade of the early 19th century was negligible, its significance as an icon of Manifest Destiny had become crucial.

MacDonald of Oregon

Tucked into the pages of Japan's history is the name Ranald MacDonald, Oregon's first ambassador to the island nation. Born at Astoria in 1824 to a British fur-trading father and Chinook mother, young Ranald's interest in Asia was piqued in 1832 when he saw three shipwrecked Japanese brought to Fort Vancouver. As he grew older, he became convinced that there was a connection between his Native American ancestry and that of the Japanese. Ranald became determined to visit the far off land.

In 1848, Ranald abandoned a whaling ship off the northern tip of Hokkaido and, pretending to be a castaway, was picked up by local fishermen. At the time, Japan was closed to all foreigners, but Ranald's Native American features allowed him to blend in with the native population. He won the trust of government officials and was soon teaching English classes in Nagasaki—the first of their kind on Japanese soil.

MacDonald's seminars were put to good use,

when in 1853, American Commodore Matthew Perry arrived in Japan to open diplomatic relations between the two nations. Two of the Japanese interpreters involved in the treaty negotiations had been students of Oregon's native son. By then, however, Ranald had left Japan. He eventually settled in British Columbia, and passed away near Fort Colville in northeastern Washington in 1894.

From Settlement to Salmon

~ 1844-1874 ~

The 1840s were a momentous period in Oregon's history. During this decade, the number of American settlers grew exponentially as overland emigrants poured into the region over the two-thousand-mile Oregon Trail. They staked claims, built homes, and in 1843, formed a provisional government. The year 1846 saw the end of joint occupancy between the British and the Americans, and two years later, Congress created the Oregon Territory. That same year, gold was discovered in California and the ensuing rush created commercial opportunities aplenty for Oregonians. Prophets and dreamers scouted the region looking for the perfect location where a great city might rise, a place where they could leave their mark, and with any luck, line their pockets.

By 1844, Oregon City seemed well on its way to becoming *the* metropolis of the Oregon Country. Situated at powerful Willamette Falls, the village was already a "city"—the first ever incorporated west of the Rockies—and the undisputed center of American activity in the region. It would be another year before Asa Lovejoy and Francis Pettygrove would flip a large copper penny to decide whether their clearing along the Willamette River would be called Boston or Portland. Some ninety miles downriver, a few optimistic souls saw the old outpost at Astoria, with its deep anchorage and ready access to the ocean, as the sure site for a great seaport.

Little remained of John Jacob Astor's settlement when John M. Shively arrived there in January of 1844. Shively, a 40-year old widower and luckless businessman, had arrived in Oregon City the previous fall as part of a wagon train known as the Great Migration. The Kentuckian decided to stake his future on Astoria. Upon landing his canoe at Fort George, Shively was greeted by Bennett O'Neal, the lone American at the outpost. Soon, O'Neal offered Shively half his unproved claim if he would put his engineering knowledge to use and survey it. Shively accepted. He went

to work running survey lines around 640 acres, which encompassed the buildings at Fort George, still occupied by the Hudson's

John Shively, settler of 1844.

Bay Company (HBC). In the process he laid out streets and developed the plat for a town, what he called the "Plan of Astoria."

Astoria, like the rest of the Oregon Country, was still under a state of joint occupancy between Great Britain and the United States. The lone British emissary at Fort George—and now an unwilling inhabitant of Shively's Astoria—was James Birnie. This listless Scot, who was not exactly a darling of the HBC, took little issue with the international interloper, though other British subjects did. But neither Royal Marines nor HBC intermediaries could oust the "imprudent Yankee," and Shively carried on with his work.

In the meantime, Shively bought O'Neal's half of the claim for $200. O'Neal, it seems, had to

In the 1850s, the area that would become downtown Astoria was part of the Columbia River. On the promontory at the top of the image can be seen the Methodist Church, the first church in Astoria, and several early homes around what is today 15th and Exchange Street.

"git" from the place to save his life after stirring up trouble with some local Native Americans.

Shively was soon joined at Astoria by another resolute frontiersman named John McClure, who proceeded to stake a claim immediately west of Shively's, stretching from what is today 13th Street west to about First Street. A wayfaring soul, McClure had left his native Kentucky for Indiana,

VIEW OF ASTORIA, OREGON.

and was at one time a resident of New Orleans before coming to the Northwest Coast by way of California. Like Shively, McClure cared little for the notion of joint occupancy, and in 1846, got in a scrape with Alexander Lattie, a newly appointed clerk at Fort George, which nearly reached a

fatal climax.

By 1845, Americans had claimed all of the land from Point George to Tongue Point. Samuel "Tickey" Smith filed papers on the western end of Astoria's peninsula, and Point George became Smith's Point. Upriver from Shively's property, east of what is now 33rd Street, a State-of-Mainer named Albert E. Wilson claimed the future site of Uppertown. Farther east yet was the land claim of the irascible Robert Shortess, the northern portion of which would become Alderbrook.

After filing his Astoria claim with the provisional government at Oregon City, John Shively headed east in late 1845. The reasons for his departure are not clear, though some say he left to retrieve his son that he had left with family in Missouri, while others contend it was because the HBC refused to sell him provisions. In either case, while in St. Louis, a government official urged him to continue on to Washington, D.C. to weigh in on the Oregon boundary issue then being debated in Congress. Shively did, and in 1846 the long-festering "Oregon Question" was settled when the two countries decided to draw the international boundary along the 49th parallel. Incidentally, after the treaty signing the HBC relocated its Pacific Northwest operations to Fort Victoria on Vancouver Island in 1849, north of the new border, at which time they formally relinquished Fort George to the Americans.

When Shively returned to Astoria in the summer of 1847, he brought with him his son, his new wife, and his commission as postmaster from President James K. Polk. He promptly opened up the first post office west of the Rocky Mountains, on what became 15th Street between Exchange Street and Franklin Avenue. For the next six years, mail from Astoria's regional distribution center was dispersed throughout what was to become Oregon, Washington, Idaho, and Montana.

The Astoria that Shively returned to looked more like a young settlement than the dilapidated fur trading post he had left scarcely two years previous. From four log cabins the town had grown to 10 houses, some even built of sawn lumber. Perhaps the nicest dwelling belonged to James and Nancy Welch. To Shively's surprise, in his absence Welch had taken charge of his claim. How Welch came into possession of Shively's land is a matter of speculation, but a long-running dispute ensued, and a settlement was only reached after the property was divided years later. Other Astorians who arrived during Shively's absence included David Ingalls and family, as well as Ezra Fisher, a Baptist minister whose house Shively bought upon his return.

On April 3, 1849, John Adair, another Kentuckian, landed in Astoria with an appointment from President Polk to become the first U.S. Customs collector on the Pacific Coast. Adair tried fruitlessly to get the Astorians to donate land for a customs house, or even sell it at a reasonable figure, so he decided to locate on Albert Wilson's claim at Upper Astoria. He operated the first customs house from his home before building

a more formal office in 1852, near what is today 34th and Marine Drive. In the meantime, Adair bought Albert Wilson's property for $600 and laid out city streets. Adair called this Astoria, insisting its downriver neighbor was Fort George.

Although only a shallow bay separated the customs house at Upper Astoria from post office at Lower Astoria, a deep rift had been created within the town. For several decades, Astoria's city fathers worked with mutual exclusivity to grow their towns (that is, both halves of Astoria), each vying to attract new settlers, businesses, and especially government patronage. In 1856, when Astoria was incorporated under the laws of the territorial legislature, it covered Shively's claim and part of the McClure claim; Adair's Astoria was excluded. The two Astorias would not be united until the summer of 1878, when a bridge finally spanned Scow Bay—the causeway became what is today Exchange Street—and would not be joined as the same municipality until 1891.

The establishment of Astoria's customs house coincided with a significant increase in river traffic. Gold had been discovered in California

scarcely a year before, and a steady stream of ships began to visit the Columbia River to ferry Oregon's goods and resources to booming Gold Rush markets. To guide this motley flock of merchant vessels safely across the river's treacherous mouth, bar pilots began to operate from Astoria. The bar pilots and customs house soon made the town a requisite stop for ships plying the river.

During the Gold Rush a number of enterprising emigrants arrived in Astoria. From New York came W.W. and Almira Raymond, Samuel and Polly McKean, and Adam and Caroline Van Dusen. The Van Dusens had first moved to Michigan, but seeking a healthier climate, ventured to Oregon. In Astoria, Mr. Van Dusen opened a store and later an insurance office, both of which prospered. Another going concern founded in 1849 was the boarding house operated by Conrad and Philipina Boelling and family. Among the many boarders to stay at the family's hostel was Captain George Flavel, who in 1854 married the innkeepers' young daughter, Mary Christina.

Boellings' hotel helped to ease the housing shortage that plagued the place. Still, many families looking to establish themselves in Astoria found temporary shelter in the Shark House, a relatively spacious log cabin built on the waterfront in 1846 by the crew of the shipwrecked *Shark*. As crude and cramped as log cabin life was for Astorians of the 1840s and 1850s, the town's beleaguered Native American population fared much worse. With their culture dashed by disease, a number of Indians took refuge in Astoria. "They often slept under the house, " recalled Caroline

Astoria's waterfront in 1855, featuring the Parker Dock between what is now 10th and 11th Streets.

1850 *Columbia*

July 3rd was a proud day in Astoria, as everyone gathered around to watch the launching of the *Columbia*, the first steamboat built on the river. *Columbia* was a double-ended, side-wheeler, 90-feet long with a 14-foot beam. With her steam up, she cast off from Astoria with two local Indians serving as pilots and arrived in Portland 24 hours later. Though she was not overly fast, and some non-Astorians claimed not overly seaworthy, she reputably made a small fortune for her owners, Captain James Frost and James Adair, taking in $25 per head or ton on her regular run between Astoria and Oregon City. The *Columbia* was a significant improvement over her wind-dependent competitors, but her reign was short-lived. Soon, faster steamers drove the *Columbia* into obscurity and in 1853 she was dismantled.

Van Dusen of her time in the Shark House, "and one night an Indian baby was born under there."

The upswing in shipping brought to Astoria by California's Gold Rush was offset by the departure of most of the town's able-bodied men. Settlement plans were laid aside as men like John Shively, James Welch, and John Adair scurried to California. Most returned the following year with little material reward, but carried with them grander ambitions for Astoria's future. Adair, along with Captain James Frost, looked to get in on shipping and hurriedly laid the keel for a river steamer they christened *Columbia*. Welch put up a steam saw-mill with a mind to feed the lumber-hungry San Francisco markets. A few years later Wilder W. Parker bought Welch's plant and extended a wharf out into the river. The dock had just enough frontage to load a single ship, but was considered a substantial improvement as it was Astoria's first.

Among Astoria's most industrious residents of the 1850s was Judge Cyrus T. Olney. In 1857, he bought John McClure's land claim and set to work developing it. Olney had 40 acres of forestland slashed and city lots staked off. Instead of selling the parcels outright, the enterprising counselor devised what has become known as Olney's Lottery. For $50 a participant could buy a ticket that guaranteed them a lot, to be chosen at random, and entered them in the running for the grand prize of two lots, one of which included a house. The lottery did not make Olney rich but he managed to move a considerable number of lots. Olney gave land speculation another try shortly before his death in 1870, when he acquired a tract along Youngs River, where the town that bears his name now stands.

In the early 1860s, the seemingly distant Civil War brought a burst of economic activity to Astoria. To protect the Columbia River from Confederate raiders, the United States Army began construction on an earthwork fort at Point Adams in 1863. Astoria became the hub of military shipping, landing both troops and supplies for the project. Before the war was over, Union troops also built a battery atop Cape Hancock, known to civilians as Cape Disappointment, that later took the name Fort Canby.

Census takers enumerated 639 Astorians in 1870. It had been a slow three decades of growth since John Shively first landed at Fort George in 1844, but the town was on the verge of incredible expansion. In 1874, a salmon cannery was built along the town's waterfront and within a decade over half of the canneries on the lower Columbia would be located there. John Jacob Astor's western fur emporium would soon become the "Salmon Canning Capital of the World."

Government

1818-1846	The Oregon Country held under "joint oc- cupancy" between Great Britain and the United States. The British Hudson's Bay Company becomes the de facto authority in the region.
1843	Oregonians organize provisional government at Champoeg Meeting.
1844	Clatsop County created. Lexington, at present-day Warrenton, named county seat.
1848	U.S. Congress creates the Oregon Territory.
1854	By countywide vote, Astoria is made seat of county government. John McClure donates land for courthouse at 8th and Commercial.
1856	Astoria incorporated by act of territorial legislature; 20 years later, city chartered and boundaries enlarged.
1859	Oregon becomes 33rd state of the Union.

Smoky Sunset on the Columbia River, 1884
Cleveland Rockwell

COLUMBIA RIVER MARITIME MUSEUM

The Graveyard of the Pacific

Galena Stranded Clatsop Beach, Or.
Nov. 13-06, Woodfield Photo.

"The Britisher's in trouble, sir," shouted the lookout from his perch on the Boston ship *Convoy* as she lay at anchor in Baker's Bay. The little schooner had just entered the Columbia River on that historic March day in 1829, ahead of the Hudson's Bay Company brig *William and Ann*, when the wind began to pick up. The lookout gazed through the distant breakers as Captain Hanwell tried to right the foundering *William and Ann* but the currents had hold of her. She struck a shoal and was pummeled by the surf. None of her crew survived.

William and Ann was the first ship recorded lost on the Columbia River bar, a river entrance that has claimed an estimated 2,000 vessels and nearly as many souls. The Graveyard of the Pacific, as the area around this tumultuous merging of river and ocean is sometimes called, stretches from Leadbetter Point in the north, south to Tillamook Head, and upriver as far as Astoria. The broken masts and bare ribs of the Graveyard's lost ships became memorials for those who perished and warning signs to all others who plied these waters.

*One of the finest tall ships to carry grain from Portland was the **Galena**, a British-owned bark built in 1890. In November of 1906, as she lay off the bar waiting for a pilot, the rough weather carried her ashore. The 292-foot vessel became a popular tourist attraction, but within a couple of years she was swallowed by the sands of Clatsop Spit. (CCHS 7152.350)*

The sands and sediments of a watershed encompassing over a quarter of a million square miles accumulate near the Columbia's mouth as they filter into the abyssal Pacific Ocean. Before great boulder-mound jetties were installed around the turn of the 20th century, the bar was five miles wide and filled with shifting shoals and unreliable channels. Navigational charts could become dangerously inaccurate in only a few months time.

"Mere description can give little idea of the terrors of the bar of the Columbia," reported Lieutenant Charles Wilkes, leader of the United States Exploring Expedition, which charted the river's entrance in 1841. The bar, said Wilkes, was "…one of the most fearful sights that can possibly meet the eye of the sailor." He had good reason to make such a claim. The brig *Peacock*, one of the ships in Wilkes' expedition, ran aground on the sand spit that now bears her name and was pounded to bits by the surf. Unlike the crew of the *William and Ann*, all aboard the *Peacock* made it to safety.

Some crewmen on the magnificent old China liner *Great Republic* were not so fortunate. The 378-foot, side-wheeler was inbound from San Francisco in the pre-dawn of April 19, 1879, when she struck Sand Island. Her nearly 900 passengers were transferred to rescue boats as the captain and crew waited onboard for a chance to re-float the vessel. A high tide and heavy surf drove her higher on the spit, and as she began to break up, the captain ordered the *Great Republic* abandoned. In their escape a lifeboat capsized and 11 sailors drown. Decades later, wreckage from the once-proud ship was still visible on what had become Republic Spit.

Even before the *Great Republic* disaster, navi-

gational aids had been put in place to assist in safe passage over the bar. Buoys were installed to delineate the passable channels. Then, in 1856, crews completed work on a lighthouse high atop Cape Disappointment, though the project had been greatly delayed when the bark *Oriole*, carrying supplies and workers to the site, sank on the bar. Lighthouses also took shape at Point Adams in 1875, on Tillamook Rock in 1881, and at North Head in 1898.

Well outside the river's mouth, lightships were moored to act as guiding beacons to incoming vessels. In 1892, *Columbia Lightship No. 50* became the first of four such vessels to be stationed off the coast over the next 87 years. The last of the line, *WLV-604*, is now a popular attraction at the Columbia River Maritime Museum in Astoria.

Despite these navigational aids, major shipwrecks on the bar, though increasingly rare, occurred well into the 20th century. For mariners in distress, some consolation could be taken in the fact that a brave core of rescuers was always on the ready. Lifesaving stations have been in operation around the mouth of the Columbia River since 1877, though organized volunteer efforts began a decade earlier. The first official lifesaving station was located at Fort Canby, now the site of the United States Coast Guard Station Cape Disappointment.

"Cape D" as its known among those who serve there, is home to the Coast Guard's National Motor Lifeboat School, where attendees are instructed in the proper handling of the 47- and 52-foot rescue boats. These self-righting, steel-hulled vessels are a far cry from the revamped lifeboat first used to pull drowning sailors from the froth in 1867. It is perhaps inevitable that during this long span of lifesaving, death has visited the ranks of Coastguardsmen serving on the bar. In January of 1961, one of the worst incidents in Coast Guard history occurred when three of its boats, including the 52-foot *Triumph*, were lost in the attempt to rescue the Ilwaco-based crab boat *Mermaid*. In all, seven lives were lost. A few years later, Air Station Astoria came online and since that time helicopters have become a regular component of the search and rescue operations.

Read More…
One of the most vivid and well-organized books on shipwrecks at the mouth of the Columbia River is James A. Gibbs' Pacific Graveyard, first published in 1950 by Portland's Binford & Mort. Also of interest is a collection of newspaper accounts of the many tragedies and near misses on the bar compiled by Liisa Penner in her book Salmon Fever: River's End (Portland: Frank Amato Publications, Inc., 2006).

Peter Iredale

The most visited shipwreck on the West Coast is the **Peter Iredale.** Entombed in the Graveyard of the Pacific since 1906, the barnacle-encrusted bones of this four-masted steel bark are hardly recognizable as those of a once-grand sailing ship today. Still, the wreck is a picturesque reminder of the toll this notorious stretch of water once inflicted on shipping.

The 287-foot *Peter Iredale* was launched in England in 1890, and named after her primary owner, a Liverpool shipping magnate. For nearly two decades the ship regularly called on the Columbia River, and was lying just off the river's mouth when disaster struck. In the pre-dawn hours of October 25, 1906, the ship's captain lost his bearings in the squally weather, and before he could correct the *Peter Iredale*'s position, found his vessel surrounded by breakers. She struck Clatsop Beach with a terrific impact that sent the upper masts and rigging raining down on the crew. Miraculously, no one was injured.

By daylight, lifesaving crews had arrived to ferry the *Peter Iredale*'s crew ashore. The last off was her skipper, Captain Lawrence, who clutched in his hands the ship's logbook, a sextant, and a jug of whiskey. Once safely on Clatsop Beach, the captain—a dapper, middle-aged Englishman—turned to his ship, saluted, and declared "May God Bless you…and may your bones bleach in the sands." After a moment of reflection, Captain Lawrence turned to offer thanks to his rescuers and crewmen. He then placed the bottle of whiskey at their feet, and with a welcoming gesture announced, "Boys, have a drink."

Coe. Photo.

Taming the Bar

When the South Jetty was completed in 1894, it was the largest public works project of its kind in the United States. It had taken nearly a decade to complete, but the five-mile long ridge of massive boulders stretching seaward from Point Adams worked superbly. The jetty had closed the river's mouth by a mile, and created a funnel that at once stabilized and deepened the main entrance channel. It was by all accounts a marvel of engineering.

Improving the bar had been a much-discussed topic among Oregonians for decades. Losing ships and their crews because of shifting channels was unacceptable, Oregonians agreed, if something could be done about it. They began to lean on Congress, and in 1884, the first federal monies arrives through the Rivers and Harbors Bill. Subsequent appropriations allowed work to begin on a massive scale.

Boulders from upriver quarries were barged to transfer docks near Fort Stevens where they were loaded onto railcars. From there, small steam locomotives hauled rock-laden gondolas over a trestle built along the jetty's course and the boulders were cast off either side. As the stones settled, the jetty rose above the waterline. In the years following its initial completion, more work was done to the South Jetty, and by 1914 it reached nearly seven miles in length.

Although the jetty succeeded in opening the south channel, it directed much of the river's sediment to the north shore where it began to pile up. The Corps of Engineers decided to build a north jetty, upon which work commenced in 1914. Built in a similar fashion to its southern mate, the two-mile-long North Jetty was finished two years later. Now, funneled by a jetty on each extreme, the river split Peacock Spit and scoured the ship channel to a depth that would accommodate even the deepest-draft vessels of the time.

Painting by Cleveland Rockwell

Courage and Commerce
The Columbia River Bar Pilots

Although jetties and dredging have greatly improved the shipping channel traversing the Columbia River bar, they have not managed to alleviate the fog, wind, river currents, and ocean tides. These variables can yield disaster for even the most well equipped craft. But here ships' masters rely on Columbia River Bar Pilots, who for over a century and a half have guided vessels across the river's unruly entrance.

Every major harbor has some form of pilot service, but none face the same challenges as those who navigate ships the 17 nautical miles between

Bar pilots of the 1850s: A. C. Farnsworth, J. G. Hustler, Charles Edwards, Moses Rogers, and Alfred Crosby.

the ocean and Astoria. Over the years, about two-dozen pilots have died on the job, the most recent in 2006.

Early ship captains employed Native Americans to identify the passable channels through the most treacherous stretches of river, including the bar. In 1846, the Oregon provisional government created a bar pilot licensing program and a few months later appointed the first pilot, Selah C. Reeves. In his short tenure as pilot, Reeves faired poorly, though no one doubted his courage or ambition. After running the Hudson's Bay ship *Vancouver* aground, he was accused of pilfering its goods and had his commission revoked in the summer of 1848.

By 1850, Jackson G. Hustler and Cornelius White, former pilots on New York Harbor, had been granted pilot licenses. The pilots boarded

inbound vessels while still in the ocean, via their 64-foot schooner *Mary Taylor*, and commanded the ships through the restless bar before they disembarked at Astoria. Similarly, outbound ships were boarded at Astoria, guided across the bar, and the pilots returned on the schooner.

The *Mary Taylor* has long since been replaced by a host of pilot boats, but the method of getting the pilots to and from ships remained largely unchanged. *Columbia* has been the most popular name for boats tasked with this chore. In recent times, the bar pilots have also started using a helicopter, the *Seahawk*, to deliver their members to inbound ships.

If conditions on the bar become too savage, pilots will suspend their service, which is an indication to all that the portal is closed to traffic. It is a decision they do not take lightly. For bulk carriers, like grain and logs ships, a closure of the bar is not inordinately critical, but to vessels classed as "liner-service," typically those that carry cars and containers, a rigid schedule must be maintained. A delayed bar crossing for these craft can create a ripple in commerce felt worldwide.

(Captain Robert Johnson Photo, Courtesy of the Columbia River Maritime Museum)

Around 1915, Captain George Gunderson founded what became the current Columbia River Bar Pilots Association. In 1956, the group formed a closed corporation with the pilots dividing the shares. Today, the association is comprised of 16 pilots who are at the top of their field, each with at least two year's experience sailing as a master with an unlimited license at the helm of an ocean-going vessel. In keeping with the times, in 1994 Captain Deborah Dempsey became the first female Columbia River Bar Pilot.

Captain George Flavel

The early history of the Columbia River bar pilots' association is largely the story of George Flavel. The Captain's success at organizing and managing the group led to his three-decade reign as the gatekeeper of the Columbia. Over that time, numerous attempts were made to wrest control of the pilot service from Flavel, but on every occasion he outmaneuvered his rivals. "Captain George Flavel was a man who could master Fate," said his widow Mary years after his death. "Other men had equal opportunities but he made the most of his and bent conditions to his profit."

Profits from Flavel's bar pilot service were handsome, and so too were the returns from his other business interests. During his lifetime he owned several ships, but none as swift or lucrative as the barkentine Jane A. Falkenberg. On the river, Flavel operated numerous steam-powered towboats. In downtown Astoria, he put up the grand Occident Hotel in 1869, and along the

waterfront oversaw his busy warehouse and wharf. In 1882, Flavel purchased several thousand acres at Tansy Point, across Youngs Bay from Astoria, which he later sold to developers who drew up plans for a projected city they called Flavel.

For four decades, Captain George Flavel was Astoria's most well known resident, yet few Astorians knew him. Some graciously excused his aloofness on account of his "proud and reticent nature," while others simply considered him "a grave saturnine sphinx; sour, dour, cold and crabbed." This guarded persona has made the tall, bewhiskered captain a most curious subject for historical inquiry.

Flavel never offered the particulars of his early life and none dared ask. It is believed that he was born in Norfolk, Virginia, though some sources suggest New Jersey, or even Ireland. The first sure facts of Flavel's life emerge 25 years later, when he arrived in Astoria as master of his own ship. That was in 1849, and after sailing in the coast trade

between San Francisco and the Columbia River, he made Astoria his permanent home in the early 1850s. On March 26, 1854, he married Mary Christina Boelling, the 14-year-old daughter of a prominent local family. Ten months later she gave birth to a son, George Conrad. Soon, daughters Nellie and Katie joined the family.

Tending to business affairs demanded most of Flavel's energy, yet he found time to serve his adopted home. In the 1870s and 1880s, he was county treasurer, a school board member, city councilman, and Clatsop County commissioner. He died on July 3, 1893. In 1936, the late Captain's great-granddaughter, Patricia Jean Flavel, donated the family's elaborate 1885 Victorian mansion to the city. Today, the house is maintained in its original splendor by the Clatsop County Historical Society.

At rest on Astoria's waterfront is the pilot boat Joseph Pulitzer.

The Steamboat Era

Before the automobile, communities along the lower Columbia River were linked by water. Rivers and bays were not hindrances to be bridged or skirted, but the very highways on which freight, mail, and passengers moved. Beginning in the 1850s, and for some eight decades to follow, steamboats both large and small ruled these waters. Attentive residents along the lower Columbia knew each boat by its whistle, and their comings and goings were part of daily life.

Inset: Known for her swiftness and elegance, the sternwheeler Telephone plied the lower Columbia River for several decades beginning in the 1880s. She spent her later years as a ferry in San Francisco. (Courtesy of the Columbia River Maritime Museum, CRMM 570-13292)

Background: The R. Miler pulls away from Astoria on her way to across the Columbia River. (CCHS 5284.349)

The pioneer steamboat on the Columbia River was the *Beaver*, a small side-wheeler that arrived at Fort Vancouver in 1836 as part of the Hudson's Bay Company fleet. The first American steamer to ply the river was Astoria's own *Columbia*, built in 1850. Steam navigation on the river expanded rapidly, and in 1854, John Ainsworth and Jacob Kamm introduced the stern-wheeler design to the waters of the Columbia Basin when the *Jennie Clark* slid down the ways and into the Willamette River.

In 1860, Ainsworth, Kamm, and other prominent upriver businessmen formed the Oregon Steam Navigation Company, which for nearly two decades enjoyed a monopoly on steamboat navigation between Astoria and The Dalles. Within a couple years, the *Jennie Clark* began weekly summertime service transporting affluent Portlanders to and from the coast. During the 1870s and 1880s, Seaside became the destination of choice for many vacation-minded Oregonians, and to carry them on their travels came a host of stately steamers.

Among the leaders in the tourist trade were Captain U. B. Scott's sternwheelers *Telephone* and *Bailey Gatzert*, which were as grand as they were fast. The *Telephone*, old rivermen claimed, was the fastest of her kind ever built. In the summer of 1884, she made the Portland to Astoria run in just over four and a half hours. The *Baily Gatzert*, built in Ballard, Washington in 1890 and named after one of Seattle's early mayors, cruised the river from the 1890s until 1918. She later served as an automobile ferry on Puget Sound before being decommissioned in 1926.

Arguably the plushest steamer to call on As-

River steamers like the R. Miler and Julia B., seen here along Astoria's waterfront in the early 1900s, were an essential transportation link for isolated communities on the Columbia's north shore like Knappton, Deep River, and Cathlamet. (CCHS 451.340)

toria was the *T. J. Potter*, a 230-foot side-wheeler. Her grand mahogany bar, oversized mirrors, and elegant staterooms were accompanied by a host of Victorian-era affectations. Built in 1888, the graceful *Potter* ferried tourists until 1916. She was then used sporadically for menial jobs until 1925, when she was towed to the mud flats along Youngs Bay and burnt so her metal fittings could be gathered. It is said that at low tide her ribs can still be seen protruding from the muck not far from Tapiola Park.

During the *T. J. Potter's* active life, one of her stops was at Megler, on the Washington shore, where she met the little trains of the Ilwaco Railroad & Navigation Company. This narrow gauge railroad took passengers and freight from the wharf to waypoints all along the North Beach Peninsula as far as Nahcotta. Then as now, the peninsula was a popular summer destination. Besides the *Potter*, tourists arrived at the railhead on the steamers *Ocean Wave*, *Nahcotta*, and *Canby*.

By the turn of the 20th century, Astoria was home to an assortment of smaller steamboats that served settlements along both shores of the big river. These boats were the only regular connection to the outside world for north shore communities like Altoona, Grays River, Deep River, and Knappton. On these runs, the *Shamrock*, *General Washington*, *Juilia B.*, and many others carried mail, passengers, and freight to the remote hamlets.

By the 1930s, the era of the riverboats was at its end. The *Georgiana* and *America* were among the last of their kind to have a regularly scheduled service to Astoria. By then, however, the ever-developing highway system had eclipsed this historic form of transportation.

The Shipbuilders

For United States Shipping Board of P.C.
McEachern
Hull No. 6
Feb. 2 19..

A rich tradition of wood crafting exists in and around Astoria. Fashioning objects from this abundant resource has been a part of the area's culture since ancient times. The most skilled practitioners of this art—whether they employed stone tools or electric implements—were those who built boats.

For millennia, Native Americans hewed and burned and bent great cedar logs to form their canoes. Euro-American boat building techniques arrived in the Pacific Northwest in the spring of 1811 with the first Astorians. While erecting their outpost, the company's carpenters also assembled a small sailboat, the parts for which had been brought around the Horn in the *Tonquin*. *Dolly*, as the little schooner was named, became the first American vessel launched on the Pacific Coast.

In 1850, the first steamboat built on the Columbia River slid down the ways at Astoria, though the town's boat building tradition did not truly begin for several decades to come. One of the earliest boat shops belonged to Richard Benjamin and Joseph Leathers, who opened a plant at the foot of 4th Street in 1872. They did a brisk business crafting fishing vessels and river steamers, and they were certainly not alone. During the waning decades of the 19th century, Astoria's boatyards turned out hundreds of gillnet boats and many larger fishing craft, utility boats, and even tall ships.

One of Astoria's leading boatbuilding firms belonged to Finnish immigrant brothers Carl, Frans, and Frithiof Kankkonen. Carl had already taken the name Charles Wilson by the time he arrived in Astoria in 1885. Here he busied himself gillnetting, and in the offseason working as a carpenter. Eight years later, Frans—who retained the family's

surname—joined Charles in Astoria, and together they began fabricating boats and buildings. They helped build several salmon canneries in Uniontown, and in 1902, built the Taylor School. As the schoolhouse walls were going up, their youngest brother, Frithiof, arrived in town. Together they operated Wilson Brothers' Shipyard at Smiths Point.

The First World War brought Astoria its greatest shipbuilding boom. Three major shipyards hurried to construct vessels for the U. S. Shipping Board during the war: Rogers Shipbuilding at the Port of Astoria's Pier 2, McEachern Ship Company on Youngs River, and Wilson Shipbuilding at Smiths Point. Just before America's entry into the war, the Wilson Brothers' Shipyard was reorganized as Wilson Shipbuilding, a corporation headed by some of the lower Columbia's most prominent lumbermen including Peter J. Brix, founder of the Knappton Towboat Company. According to J. Marlene Eskola Taylor, a Wilson descendent, Wilson Shipbuilding employed nearly 1,000 men during these peak years, as Astoria's population doubled during the shipbuilding flurry of 1917-1918.

With the cessation of hostilities, the government issued stop work orders for Astoria's wartime shipyards in early 1919. Just as quickly as it had blossomed, the town's shipbuilding industry withered. The Rogers and McEachern yards soon closed, and Wilson Shipbuilding continued for only a decade more, building mainly tugboats and trollers.

War would again revive Astoria's shipbuilding industry in the 1940s. The firm at the center of much of the activity was the Astoria Marine Construction Company (AMCO), which was founded

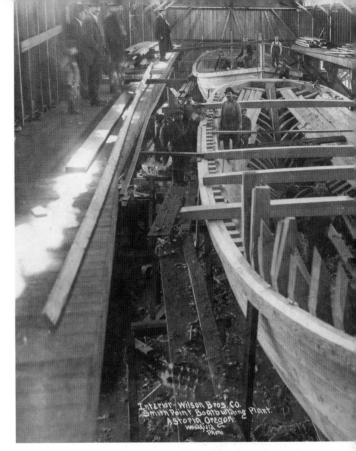

Interior-Wilson Bros. Co.
Smith Point Boatbuilding Plant.
Astoria, Oregon.

in 1925 by Joseph Dyer. Located along the Lewis and Clark River, AMCO built fishing vessels and yachts prior to the Second World War, then turned out 39 minesweepers and auxiliary vessels for the government during the early 1940s.

AMCO is still in the marine repair business as are a number of other local firms, but ships no longer take shape along Astoria's waterfront. Today, one of the most noticeable relics of those bygone days are the long, sloping rows of piling jutting off Smiths Point, the rotting ways that once carried the great wooden vessels from the Wilson Shipbuilding yards into Youngs Bay.

The Port
of ASTORIA

In the 1920s, promoters with grandiose intentions began billing Astoria as "The Future New York City of the Pacific." It is perhaps inevitable considering the city's location at the confluence of a mighty river and great ocean, that its boosters would from time to time nurture visions of it becoming a leading regional seaport. It was self-evident, they declared, that the Columbia River basin was a great natural funnel where resources of all kinds would inherently flow to this central point at the river's mouth for shipment around the globe.

Unfortunately for Astoria, geography and the economies of transportation favored an upriver site as Oregon's shipping center. Still, the town possessed a fine harbor and was rich with its own commodities, especially salmon and timber. Lumber ships began calling on Astoria in the 1850s, and by the 1880s canned salmon ranked as the leading export. For a time, grain barged from the Willamette Valley was loaded on ocean-going vessel at Astoria's Farmer's Dock, though a lack of financing soon thwarted the enterprise.

The steady growth in shipping and the much-anticipated opening of the Panama Canal led to the creation of The Port of Astoria in 1910. Set up as a municipal corporation controlled by five commissioners, its purpose was to promote Clatsop County's maritime and commercial interests. In 1914, the port began an ambitious reclamation project of intertidal mud flats along Taylor Avenue in Uniontown. Commissioners issued millions of dollars worth of bonds, purchased the study dredge

Natoma, and put an army of contractors to work. Three large marine terminals began to take shape.

Improvements came rapidly to the port. Crews drove thousands of piling, installed seawalls, and with the dredge *Natoma* filled in the area between the slips. From a railroad switchyard, spur tracks threaded onto each pier, giving shippers transcontinental rail access over the Spokane, Portland & Seattle Railway. An enormous warehouse soon

went up paralleling Pier 1. Appropriately, the port's first customer was a salmon cannery that rented warehouse space for 100 tons of canned product, and the first cargo to leave the docks was canned salmon as well.

In 1917, a monstrous grain elevator and flourmill took shape. The towering cement structures quickly became the port's most recognizable feature and ranked among its busiest too. But after

a long and useful life, the flourmill was closed in the 1970s. When it was deemed structurally unsound in the mid-1980s, demolition experts were brought in to level the landmark. As the thunderous charges went off great clouds of dust and smoke filled the air. When the pall cleared, the flourmill still stood. Chagrined, the explosives experts tried again, but with the same result. Again and again they tried to blow the building and on the eighth day they rested. Finally, on the night of February 16, 1986 the old flourmill collapsed on its own accord.

According to historian Russell Dark, the golden age of shipping for the Port of Astoria spanned from the mid-1920s until World War II. During this period, the docks hummed as longshoremen jockeyed cargos of wheat, canned salmon, lumber, and coal on and off merchant ships. In the 1920s, declares Historian Dark, it was not uncommon for a dozen ships per week to call on the port.

Maritime commerce was not the Port's only ambition. In the 1930s, with funding from the Public Works Administration, the port and several other municipal entities began developing an airport across Youngs Bay from Astoria within the city of Warrenton. At the airfield's opening ceremony in 1936, one of its staunchest advocates, County Judge Guy Boyington, was honored and today the facility bears his name.

of *Fish* and *Forest*

Fisherman Jalmar Wilson holds his prized 82½-pound Chinook salmon caught off Astoria, May 26, 1936. The Union Fishermen's Co-operative Packing Company sent the whopper packed in ice to President Franklin D. Roosevelt. (CCHS 7061.320)

LÄNNEN UUTISET.
FINNISH & ENGLISH JOB PRINTING.

Fred Karinen

Lännen Uutiset

JOB PRINTING.

KIRJAPAINOTYÖTÄ.

Finnish immigrant Fred Karinen's print shop is an example of one of many lines of work Astoria's immigrants found outside of the traditional occupations of fishing, logging, and farming. (CCHS 7984.400)

"In and around Astoria, at one time, were approximately four hundred men, each of whom was called John Johnson. They were not all born that way; their names were manufactured from whole cloth. Among them were Swedes, Danes, Norwegians, Finns, Russians, Poles, and even Chinese. John Johnsons, every one … As immigrants fresh from the Old Country, they were named John Johnson by employers who could not spell or pronounce many foreign names, or at least would not attempt to."

— Stewart H. Holbrook,
Far Corner (1952)

Alderbrook's "Hindu Alley" is seen in the foreground amid the other housing for workers at the nearby Hammond Sawmill. Indian immigrants, sometimes called "Hindoos" by the local newspapers, resided in these dwellings for the first couple of decades of the 20th century. (CCHS 6816.906)

Whether their name was Johnson, Rouhoja, Tarabochia, or Chan, Astorians have long represented a rich blend of cultures and ethnicities. Like all immigrants, they left ancestral homes to seek new opportunities. Their letters home told of the promise of this new country and convinced their extended families and fellow countrymen to join them. Once in Astoria, they found ready employment pulling nets and oars, swinging axes and hammers, wringing laundry and packing cans. Though they came from many nations, Astoria's immigrants were united by hard work. Like the many fishers who came to call the place home, Astoria became stubborn and independent, accustomed to good seasons and bad, and ready for any kind of weather.

Astoria's diversity has been present since its founding. An assortment of Americans, British and French Canadians, and Hawaiians composed the first occupants of John Jacob Astor's trading post in 1811. A number of the fur traders found wives among the Clatsops and Chinooks. Later settlers, too, took Native American brides and these ancient cultures continued to play a role in the community's activities. As Astoria passed from a fur-trading post into a town, most of its early citizens were native-born Americans. Some came from the southern and midwestern states, though the majority were Yankees. English was their native tongue, and common among many were ancestral ties to the British Isles.

The salmon-canning bonanza that commenced

in the 1870s brought with it a wealth of new faces. Astoria became a seasonal boomtown, as every spring thousands of fishermen and cannery workers crowded the town with the coming of the salmon. A number of these transient toilers decided to stay. According to Astorian Alfred A. Cleveland, between 1874 and 1876 the town's population almost doubled, totaling nearly 2,000 inhabitants. By 1880, census returns confirmed that it was Oregon's second most populous city, ranking only behind Portland, a position that Astoria would hold until the early 1900s.

Asian workers paste "Cape Brand" labels on canned salmon at a Columbia River Packers Association plant in Astoria. (CCHS 152.330)

Chinese Cannery Workers

The earliest distinct ethnic group to be drawn by Astoria's piscatorial wealth was the Chinese.

The hands that had built the western railroads and panned gold in remote streams were now busied processing salmon. Cannery bunkhouses overflowed with Chinese laborers, most of whom were young, single men. Though written and unwritten laws forbade them from fishing, the Chinese formed the principle labor source in packinghouses along the lower Columbia River. Cannery workers were so uniformly Chinese, in fact, that in the early 1900s when a fish-processing machine was developed, it was unabashedly called the "Iron Chink."

Astoria was something of a safe haven for the Chinese in a region that by the 1880s had grown hostile toward their existence. Competition with white workers for jobs had spawned anti-Chinese sentiment in other parts of the West, eventually leading to the Chinese Exclusion Act of 1882

that, among other restrictions, outlawed their immigration. But in Astoria, where their labor was absolutely critical to the canning industry, the Chinese found relatively little acrimony. In 1880, census takers enumerated 2,122 Chinese in Clatsop County alone. As their numbers grew, a small Chinatown developed along Bond Street and its residents began organizing fraternal organizations called "tongs."

Though most remembered for their contribution in the canneries, Chinese workers also filled a number of key positions in Astoria's service economy. Some operated truck gardens within the city limits. Eino "Lank" Koskela recalled these vegetable growers peddling their goods door-to-door, conversing with Uniontown residents in Finnish. Other Chinese worked as merchants, cooks, laundrymen, tailors, barbers, and butchers.

Still, their primary occupation was in the canneries, and as the number of packinghouses began to decline in the early 1900s, so too did Astoria's Chinese population. To this day, there are still families in town that can trace their Asian ancestry back to great salmon canning days of the 19th century.

Fishers from Europe

By the 1880s, catching fish was largely the task of European immigrants. Some of the most capable fishers emigrated from the region surrounding the Adriatic Sea where casting nets had been a part of traditional culture for centuries. Many were "ichs" from the Yugoslavian states—Draglolich, Marincovich, Zankich—who located around Scow Bay, just east of the downtown district. Among the outstanding members of Astoria's Slavic community was Pete Cosovich, a well-respected businessman and civic leader who served two terms as mayor in the 1950s.

Outnumbering Astoria's Greek, Italian, and Yugoslav population were immigrants from Scandinavia. The 1860 U. S. Census recorded nine Swedes, four Norwegians, and three Danes residing in Astoria. From this modest count, Astoria's Scandinavian population would snowball, with the peak years of immigration spanning from 1890 to 1910. These immigrants found the area to have many desirable and familiar environmental attributes, not least of which were the prodigious salmon runs. Many of these foreigners had came from the coastal regions of their home countries where they had been accustomed to fishing, logging, and small-scale farming, the economic staples of their new home.

Uppertown proved to be a popular location for Norwegian newcomers. Many of the men made their living on the water, and John Riswick and Chris Christensen stood among the town's leading Norse fishers. Some brought with them skilled trades, like cobbler Sven Gimre who set up a shoe store that is still in business today, 119 years later. Similarly, merchant Erik Hauke opened a general store in Uppertown in 1890, and began a family retailing tradition that lasted for a century. Norwegian immigrants organized one of Astoria's early Lutheran churches in 1887, and in 1910 founded Nidaros Lodge No. 16 of the Sons of Norway. In 1934, the Lodge played a key roll in naming the highway through Uppertown after Viking paragon Leif Erickson.

From Sweden by way of Minnesota came Charles G. Palmberg—née—Petersson'a carpenter of unusual skill with a keen sense for business. Beginning in 1893, Charlie put up scores of residential and commercial buildings across Astoria, some of which still stand today. Benjamin and Christiana (Swanson) Young were enterprising Swedes too, and from the proceeds from his salmon canning business built one of the most elaborate mansions in town. Arguably Astoria's most notable son of Sweden was attorney Albin 'Al' Norblad. His political activities led him to

Scandinavian flags intertwine with the Stars and Stripes as these young ladies proudly display their heritage. (CCHS 6723.002)

become a state senator from 1918 until 1929, when he became governor. Norblad's son, Walter, also represented the legislative district in the state house before being elected to the U.S. Congress in 1946.

Danish immigrants made up the smallest percentage of Scandinavian immigration to Astoria, but their contribution to the place is not so easy to quantify. Beginning in the 1880s, fisherman Mathias Jensen became well known for his inventions that revolutionized the canning industry. His can-filling machine, for example, went into widespread use in packinghouses all along the Pacific Coast. Another noteworthy Dane, Oluf Petersen, labored as a logger and even worked as a shoemaker before becoming one of Astoria's leading bankers as the president of the Astoria Savings Bank.

The Finns

Astoria's largest immigrant group was Finns, and by the 1920s they comprised nearly a quarter of the town's population. The first sizeable groups of Finns began arriving in Astoria in the 1870s, and by 1888 the community could boast of a Finnish-language newspaper. The town's west end soon developed into a full-fledged Finnish enclave known as Uniontown. The name derived from a short-lived cooperative salmon packing plant, the Union Cannery, founded by thirty Finnish fishermen in 1882. Uniontown soon had a Lutheran Church and in 1886 a benevolent, fraternal society, the Finnish Brotherhood. In 1893, another social hall, Suomi Hall, was erected in Uniontown.

Many Finns clung to their traditional religious beliefs, but some began to espouse a newly attained belief in socialism. The more conservative ones became known as "Church Finns," while the socialists were dubbed "Red Finns." The latter group formed the Astoria Finnish Socialist Club in 1905 and began publishing a regional Finnish-language newspaper, the *Toveri*. Despite their political awareness and overwhelming numbers, however, Finns of either stripe served few roles in local government.

With the Finlanders came their traditional

steam bath, the sauna. A true Finn, it was said, would not let a Saturday night pass without a visit to a sauna, and for some that meant a call upon Kaarlo Koskelo's Union Steam Bath, one of Astoria's longest-lived Finnish bathhouses. Here, sauna goers would "take steam," called "loyly" in their mother tongue, while switching themselves with birch branches and socializing, before ending the session with a cold, cleansing shower.

"Hindu Alley"

The most distinct looking immigrants to arrive in Astoria were a group that locals mistakenly referred to as Hindus. They were actually Sikhs, mostly, from the Punjab region of Northern India who wore long beards and turbans as tenets of their Sikh faith. Many of these East Indians—they were almost entirely men—had left their farms and families in the face of drought and epidemics to seek new opportunities in America. In Astoria, where they began arriving around 1900, they predominately found employment in the Hammond Sawmill in Alderbrook. The cluster of mill company houses they inhabited on Birch Street, between 51st and 52nd, became known as "Hindu Alley."

The 400 or so Asian Indians who called Astoria home had limited interaction with the rest of the community. Their appearance and customs made them seem the most foreign in a town full of foreigners. Still, they had a great deal in common with other expatriates, especially the Finns. India, like Finland, had long been provinces of an imperial power—for the Finns it was Russia, while for the Indians it was Britain. According to Kar Dhillon, a Sikh born in Astoria in 1915, the Gadar Party, an Indian freedom-fighting organization,

Among Astoria's successful Chinese merchants was Wah Sing, a tailor and owner of a men's clothing store, seen here with his wife, Quan Tai, and family around 1900. (CCHS 139.00S)

was founded in Astoria two years before her birth. Within a few years, the call to fight for Indian independence had spurred the "Hindu" exodus from Astoria, and by the time the Hammond Sawmill burnt in 1922, few East Indians remained within the city.

For decades, much of Astoria's growth and prosperity was the work of its immigrants. By 1940, though, over 82 percent of Astoria's population was native-born Americans. The sons and daughters of the immigrants shed their parents' native tongue and, more often than not, had little use for their old world customs. The era of the pseudo John Johnsons has long since passed, but the legacy of Astoria's immigrants lives on in the spirit of their descendants.

Piscatorial Wealth

BY IRENE MARTIN

When Lewis and Clark arrived on the Columbia in 1805, they marveled at the abundant runs of salmon and native reliance on them. Chinook, coho (silver), blueback (sockeye), chum (dog) and steelhead all returned at different seasons of the year, providing year-round nourishment and forming the basis of the local Native American economy and culture. Salmon is a small fraction of today's catch, but is still what lingers in the memory. The combination of history and present-day fisheries conducted, in many cases, by the descendants of early fishermen on the Columbia, gives Astoria its fishing glamour.

Removing a batch of canned salmon from the steam cooker. (CCHS 7452. 330)

Asian cannery workers ankle deep in salmon. Chinese laborers formed the primary labor source in canneries all along the lower Columbia until the early decades of the 1900s. (CCHS 5613.330)

After Lewis and Clark and their company returned home, anticipation ran high that the West Coast would be a rich source for furs. The John Jacob Astor Expedition led to the founding of Astoria in 1811. The Columbia's two major fur-trading companies were the Northwest Company and the Hudson's Bay Company (HBC), which merged in 1821. The HBC diversified by engaging in the salt salmon trade, as correspondence and numerous entries in the logs of company vessels attest.[1] James Birnie and other company employees at Ft. George processed quantities of the oil-rich large summer Chinook for export to Hawaii, China, and other parts of the U.S. Good quality fish generally found a market, but lack of basic sanitation standards, coupled with the scarcity of necessary supplies, such as high quality barrels and sufficient salt, frequently led to spoilage.[2]

After the 49th parallel became the official boundary between Canada and the U.S. in 1846, the HBC moved its headquarters from Ft. Vancouver to Victoria, British Columbia, effectively ending its domination of the salt salmon trade on the

Columbia River. James Birnie and his son-in-law, Alexander Anderson, continued as agents for the company, purchasing fish from local native fishers and salting it.[3]

By the early 1850s, small entrepreneurs were finding a niche along the Columbia. The native population had declined so substantially from the diseases that accompanied American and European immigration that some of the new arrivals began fishing themselves and salting salmon. In 1866 the Hume brothers began salmon canning at Oak Point on the Columbia River. Although they tried to keep their process secret, it did not take long for others to emulate their example. By the early 1870s, salmon canning had reached Astoria.

Badollet and Company began constructing the first cannery in Astoria in December 1873.[4] The May 7, 1874, *Weekly Astorian* commented that "large parties of visitors from this city have been to the upper-town cannery during the past week, and all express themselves well paid for the time spent in observing the workings of this new productive establishment, which is now in full operation."

The Adair brothers built the A. Booth and Company cannery, the second in Astoria, in 1874, naming it after their partner, Alfred Booth.[5] Eventually the Adairs established other canneries, both on the Fraser River in B.C. and on the Columbia River, and put up enormous packs of salmon. "The total pack of the two brothers within seven years [1874-1881] has been 276,000 cases, an aggregate production unsurpassed in this industry. The average annual pack of the two was nearly 40,000 cases, and each has dispatched 900 cases in a day, or more than 22 tons of cleaned fish. Their canneries are models of efficiency in convenience

Cannery workers hand packing albacore in the 1940s. (CCHS 3292.330)

of arrangement and completeness of machinery. Steam-power is used to save human labor as far as possible and applied even to such purposes as filling the cans with the pieces of salmon."[6]

Other canneries followed in Astoria in rapid succession. New cannery proprietors included John Devlin, and Robert, William, and George Hume, Watson brothers, J.O. Hanthorn, and Marshall Kinney, who built the Astoria Packing Company, one of the largest packing houses on the Columbia River. Kinney was one of the major stockholders in Columbia River Packers Association after it was formed in 1899. Henry Doyle's rich gossipy memoir describes Kinney's business dealings:

He was a man of vision who foresaw that one of the surest repositories of wealth lay in the possession of timber limits. He had no desire to operate a lumbering industry but aimed to acquire every acre of virgin timber he could afford to own and generally what he could afford was far less than he sought to possess. As a consequence he was always in need of ready money to carry his timber leases and pay their royalties and he robbed his cannery Peter to pay his timber Paul and so juggled both business undertakings that his fellow townsmen awaited from day to day the announcement, which however never came, that his financial house of cards had collapsed...."[7]

While many of the new canneries were built and operated by individuals, another factor in salmon canning was the cooperative movement. Popular in Europe, particularly in the Scandinavian countries and Finland where many local fishermen originated from, numerous cooperative ventures arose in Astoria. Some, such as the Anglo-American Packing Company, and the Eagle Packing Company, had brief life spans. Others, such as the Union Fishermen's Cooperative Packing Company, lasted well into the 20th century.

The White Star Packing Company and several other co-ops all were associated at one time or another with Cross Timmons, a fisherman from Maine who started out as a gillnetter in 1867, salting his own fish.[8]

The Columbia Cannery and the Thistle Cannery were short-term Astoria operations during the late 1870s and 1880s. The Seaside Cannery (1877-1884), the West Coast Packing Company (ca. 1880-1887), and the Washington Cannery (1882-1888) also operated for brief stints.[9] Collections in the Columbia River Maritime Museum and the Oregon Historical Society contain numerous one-of-a-kind salmon can labels, the sole evidence of companies that winked out like dying stars during the 19th century. Names unknown to us now, such as Daisy Brand, packed by Miller & Co., or Sunset Brand, by Sunset Packing Co., and numerous others show that the rags to riches stories of successful and powerful packers were not necessarily the norm. The dozens of failed companies highlight the risks in the nascent salmon canning industry. A fire that destroyed a cannery building or a spoiled pack due to poor sanitary standards were just two hazards that might terminate a business.

Over the decades, a number of Astoria's waterfront canneries met with a fiery end, including the Sanborn Cannery. (CCHS 1718.330)

But the demand for the product was huge and the pack of fish was stupendous. In the late 1870s the *New York Times* described Astoria after the world had "learned to eat canned salmon." "Half a million cases cross the Atlantic every year, and are sold in Liverpool, London and elsewhere. On the dock today there are 2,000 or more cases which will go by steamer to San Francisco, and thence by rail to New York, or by steamer to Liverpool."[10]

Each case held 48 one-pound cans, and it took about three Chinook salmon to make one case.

With the end of the 1870s the basic parameters of the canning industry were established, with owner operated or cooperative canneries being the primary business models. The Humes, who had dominated the first few years, had numerous rivals. Technological innovation in the canning process proceeded at a rapid rate. A local fishing fleet and permanent communities were developing. Struggles among packers and fishers over prices had begun, as local co-ops attested.

The formation of the Columbia River Fishermen's Beneficial Aid Society in 1875 provided a means for insuring fishermen so that their widows would receive an indemnity in case of death. It was the forerunner of the Columbia River Fishermen's Protective Union, formed in 1879, pledging to work for better prices, safety and navigation issues and conservation of salmon. In 1886 the CRFPU allied with the American Federation of Labor.[11] Gear such as seines, fishwheels, and traps set up rivalries among fishermen and also pitted fishermen against the canners, who could afford the large capital investment required by these gears.

By the mid-1870s packers had developed national and international markets and brand names to entice buyers. In the purple prose of the time, "Less than 25 years ago (in 1866) the piscatorial wealth of this noble stream was practically unknown to the world; now the name of 'Columbia River salmon' is a household word all over the civilized globe. It has met with welcome and recognition everywhere, and has given world-wide renown to this section of our country."[12] Such renown continued throughout the century, with the packers fostering the reputation of their product with prize-winning entries in competitions such as the 1893 Chicago World's Fair.

The last two decades of the 19th century brought new packers to the forefront in Astoria. These included Samuel Elmore, George H. George, William Barker, Francis Cutting and his partners, two brothers, Nathaniel and Eben Tallant, both from New England.[13] Company names included Point Adams Packing Company and New England Fish Company, known for the slogan "Packed with the wiggle in its tail," Union Fishermen's Cooperative Packing Company and the Columbia River Packers Association. These latter two companies, which lasted well into the 20th century, were quite different in their formation.

On October 12, 1896, two hundred fishermen from the Astoria area gathered together to form Union Fishermen's Cooperative Packing Company. The fishermen had held an unsuccessful two-month strike during the summer Chinook season in 1896. As fisherman Matt Korpela wrote,

"The strike with its various phases was a learning experience in the rights of the fishermen. The unanimous decision, after deliberations among the fishermen, was: 'Let's build our own cannery.'"[14] They first canned fish on April 11, 1897. The company operated as a co-op for over fifty years.[15]

The Columbia River Packers Association (CRPA) formed in 1899, consolidating the holdings of a number of packers who recognized that, given the economic conditions of the country and declining levels of salmon, the numbers of canning facilities on the river could not be sustained. The packers who sold to the new association included Aberdeen Packing Co. (B.A. Seaborg); Eureka and Epicure (William Gosslin); J.O. Hanthorn's Columbia River Canneries Co.; Fishermen's Packing Company (Gust Holmes and August Moberg); J.W. and V. Cook's plant at Clifton; Samuel Elmore's plant at Astoria; and Astoria Packing Co. (Marshall Kinney). The

The tender Leader delivers boxes of fish to a CRPA facility. (CCHS 7023.330C)

Pier 39, at the foot of 39th Street in Uppertown, is the last historic salmon cannery along Astoria's waterfront. Originally the J. O. Hanthorn Cannery, the facility served many years as a Bumble Bee Cold Storage plant.

new company also acquired can labels and brand names, among which was Bumble Bee, that later became the company's trade name.[16] By the 1960s, Bumble Bee Seafoods had become the world's largest canned salmon packer.

Twentieth century additions to the salmon canning industry included Barbey Packing Company and the Arthur Anderson Fish Company. Other salmon canning operations existed during Astoria's long love affair with the salmon industry. What made the Columbia's canning industry successful was the combination of technological innovation, such as the invention of the steam retort for cooking the cans of fish, coupled with the vast supply of salmon. Unlike packers elsewhere, canners on the Columbia could afford to experiment, since the raw material was, in the early

years at least, cheap and abundant. From here, their technological advances spread to other parts of the West Coast.

Astoria was not just the home of salmon-canning, although that is how it made its place in the history of fish processing. In the mid-1930s, changing ocean conditions brought significant numbers of albacore tuna closer to the coast. The Astoria packers began canning albacore, and their packs increased rapidly. Not only did they gain a new product, allowing them to diversify, they were able to use their plants year-round, instead of just during the salmon season. Albacore could be frozen and held, and metered out in a systematic way so that crews could work all winter packing them. Nationally known corporations such as Del Monte and Van Camp, that heretofore had not had a

presence on the Columbia, arrived to take advantage of the tuna resource. At about this time, the processors formed the Columbia Salmon and Tuna Packers Association to work on issues of fish supply, legislation, and issues that affected their businesses, particularly hydroelectric development of the Columbia River.

Crab packing was another venture that began around the time of World War II. CRPA pioneered this venture, along with New England Fish Company.[17] Limited bottom fishing began in the 1950s, although it did not expand significantly until the 1970s, after passage of the Magnuson Stevens Act in 1976. With advances in processing techniques, such as freezing, whiting, formerly known as Pacific hake, also became a sought-after species in the 1970s, with shrimp following in the

1980s. The sardine fishery is the most recent adaptation to find a home in Astoria and environs, because of the renewed presence of sardines in the area. Sardines are a salt-water fish whose populations fluctuate on a 30 to 40 year cycle, alternating with anchovies. The sardines are sold as bait in Asian markets, although experimentation with their use for human consumption is under way.[18]

In terms of seafood production today, Astoria is the 13th largest seafood port in the U.S. by volume and 23rd by value of catch.[19] The seafood industry is diverse. Homegrown operations flourish, such as the multi-generational Josephsons' Smokehouse and Dock, the family-operated Oregon Ocean Seafoods (Skipanon Brand), and Fishhawk Fisheries. In the words of Steve Fick, owner of Fishhawk, "I had fishing connections through family and saw opportunities to get into fish buying and marketing in the early 1980s. I did a lot of the work myself and kept my overhead low, and built relationships with customers." Satellite plants owned by American companies headquartered elsewhere, such as Bornstein's, and Pacific Coast, a subsidiary of The Pacific Seafood Group, and Ocean Beauty offer competition. International companies such as Da Yang Seafoods, which focuses on the export of sardines, also operate plants in the area. Ancillary businesses including marinas, gear stores, such as Englund Marine, boat repair shops, such as AMCO, machinery repair and marine electronics shops, all attest to the importance of this traditional industry. Industry associations, such as the Columbia River Fishermen's Protective Union and Salmon For All, are still active.

And the past is still present. Restored examples of the Columbia River "bowpicker," the fish

An artistic rendering of Marshall Kinney's Astoria Packing Company located at the foot of 6th Street.

boat indigenous to the Columbia, grace various sites around town. The Columbia River Maritime Museum features the salmon fishery's heyday in its Great Hall. Pier 39, a privately developed refurbishing of the former Bumble Bee Cold Storage plant, contains a small museum display of the industry. Numerous displays in local businesses attest to the salmon fishery's place in the town's image of itself. The photos of the small boats, views of the huge river, the classic pictures of sailboat days and the "butterfly fleet," men hauling seine nets by hand, and the giant Royal Chinook – all are part of the history and legend of the community that still lives on fish but has continued to expand its horizons even farther west to the Pacific Ocean and beyond.

The endnotes for "Piscatorial Wealth" can be found at the Clatsop County Historical Society's Heritage Museum.

The Gillnet

This row of classic Columbia River gillnet boats is tied between "net racks"—once a common sight on Astoria's waterfront. About once a week the fishermen would haul their nets onto these racks so that they could air dry, and if needed, be repaired. (CCHS 790.360)

The foremost piece of commercial fishing gear used on the lower Columbia River was—and still is—the gillnet. Introduced to the area in 1853 from Maine's Kennebec River, the drift gillnet consisted of a rectangular piece of webbing up to 1,800 feet in length, weighted on the lower side by a "leadline" and buoyed on top with a string of wooden corks. It was laid across a stretch of river and allowed to drift in the current. As the salmon swam into the webbing, their gills became entangled and they were caught.

Over the years, two ways of fishing gillnets

fishermen plucks a salmon from his gillnet while his "boatpuller"—a rm left over from the days of oars and sails—looks on. During the ilboat era the boatpuller rowed the boat while the skipper tended the et, but as gas-powered engines came into use, the title was used to de-ribe a gillnetter's deckhand. (Courtesy of the Columbia River Maritime useum, CRMM 167-2996)

developed. The original method involved floating the corks on top of the water, while the submerged leadline stretched the net below the surface. Later came the "diver net," with fewer corks and a heavier leadline, designed to fish on or near the river bottom. Gillnetting, by either method, was most effective at night. Prior to the 1950s, the nets' webbing was made exclusively of flax and cotton twine, which in the daylight was visible to the skittish salmon.

As the fishery developed, groups of gillnetters banded together to reserve access to particular fishing grounds, known on the Columbia as "drift rights." The notion of exclusivity to a specific stretch of river had grown out of the fishermen's cooperative efforts to clear their most productive drifts of net-snagging obstructions. Those who invested in improving the drift, it was understood, had the exclusive right to fish there.

Gillnetters fished from a boat that has become legendary. According to many qualified observers, the Columbia River gillnet boat was the most practical, durable, and handsome fishing vessel ever designed. The boats' slightly raised bow melded fluidly with its wide, V-shaped hull in a perfect unison of form and function. Its origins

A major portion of a gillnetter's time was spent mending his nets. With a wooden "needle" loaded with twine, these fishermen work to repair holes in the mesh. (Courtesy of the Columbia River Maritime Museum, CRMM 167-2988)

are a bit murky, but a U. S. Fish Commission bulletin from 1892 states that the first boat of this design was brought to the Columbia River from San Francisco by George and Robert Hume in 1869. Early gillnet boats were double-enders, generally 24 feet in length with a six to eight foot beam. They were propelled by oars and, when the wind was accommodating, sails.

In the early 1900s, gillnetters found that with only minor modification, a gasoline engine could be installed in their craft. As the years went on, horsepower was increased, the stern squared, and an aft pilothouse added. With the propeller astern, fishermen began laying and picking their nets from the bow. The boats became known as "bow pickers," though the original lines and basic design remained virtually unchanged. The wooden-hulled bow pickers would remain the gillnetters' workhorse until they were displaced in the second half of the 20th century by fiberglass and aluminum-hulled vessels.

Horse Seining

It was a spectacle that few who saw ever forgot: teams of draft horses plowing belly-deep through the waters of the Columbia, lugging a great arc of net onshore with tons of flopping salmon in its pocket. It was called horse seining, and its introduction to the lower Columbia has been attributed to Robert Hume, a pioneer salmon canner and noteworthy innovator. From its inception in the 1890s until its interdiction in 1948, this magnificently productive method of taking salmon was a common sight on sandbars and spits around Astoria.

The principles of beach seining date back to ancient times as Native Americans would employ nets woven of cedar bark to encircle fish passing through the shallows along sites like Chinook Beach. But with the coming of the horses, the scale of this archaic practice was expanded as the nets became longer and the hauls inestimably larger.

Horse seining commenced on an ebb tide, when a crew rowed a large skiff out into the Columbia and gunned it downriver, playing out net as they went. The oarsmen would eventually bring the boat and the "tail" of the seine back to

A teamster, known on the seining grounds as a "skinner," rides the "double tree" behind a team of horses. (Courtesy of the Columbia River Maritime Museum, CRMM 170-3095)

A crew of "beachcombers" collects the fruits of a seine haul on Sand Island. The men are loading the salmon into a wagon that will transfer the fish across the island to a tender boat waiting to carry the catch to canneries in Astoria. (CCHS 7344.310)

One of the last visible reminders of the great horse seining days on the Columbia River is a jag of piling sticking up from Desdemona Sands, just west of the Astoria Bridge at about mid-river. These barren posts once supported stables, bunkhouses, and a mess hall for the seiners who worked this sandy spit. Today, they serve chiefly as a perch for bald eagles and other birds that fish the very same grounds.

To prevent the salmon from escaping, the seiners tend to the "cork line," as teams of horses prepare to pull the "bunt," or midsection, of the net onto Kaboth Sands in 1914. (Courtesy of the Columbia River Maritime Museum, CRMM 170-3296)

shore, creating a giant semi-circle. Teamsters then hooked their horses to both ends of the net and proceeded to tighten the noose on the salmon. Once the seine was drawn in, "beachcombers" clad in tall waders would hurriedly collect the fish before loading the emptied net into the skiff for another layout.

The seining grounds were located at places like Peacock Spit, Sand Island, and Desdemona, Taylor, Elliot, and Kaboth Sands. Most of the sites were a mile or more from either shore and wholly submerged by the flood tide, so as the water advanced, both humans and horses would retreat to their camp built high atop piling. On these stilted little islands the horse seining crews, usually consisting of about 30 hands, and the five to seven teams of horses spent the season.

Sand Island quickly became the most sought

after seining location. The island was unique because of is elevation above the high-water mark, allowing for a longer work window between tides. Plus, the shoals along the island were a veritable salmon thoroughfare. In one day in 1933, for instance, horse seiners on the island landed 92 tons of salmon. This phenomenal fishing did not come cheap though. A military reserve since the Civil War, the federal government rented five seine sites on Sand Island to the highest bidders. Over the decades, these leases generated hundreds of thousands of dollars for the U.S. War Department, and made the island one of the most valuable parcels of fishing ground in the Pacific Northwest.

Timber

When the original Astorians arrived in 1811, they set to work carving their outpost from one of the greatest forests on earth...

Coe Photo.

(Mitch Mitchem Collection, Courtesy of the Clatsop County Historical Society)

The site was situated near the midpoint of the colossal temperate rain forest that blanketed the Pacific Coast from Northern Californian to Southeastern Alaska and inland to the Cascade Mountains. Along the coast, spruce and hemlock grew big and thick, while a few miles inland, Douglas-fir stretched skyward some 300 feet and Western red cedar swelled to girths sometimes in excess of 20-feet.

Ever since spike-shod loggers took to the woods, Astoria has been at the center of the area's forest economy. The town's waterfront sawmills brought windjammers and steamships to carry cargoes of lumber to ports around the Pacific and beyond. Swarms of towboats ferried giant log rafts from booms on Blind Slough, Youngs River, and elsewhere to upriver sawmills, while river steamers carried freight and passengers to logging settlements on both sides of the Columbia. Astoria's blacksmiths and machinists were kept busy hammering out the hardware used in the loggers' trade, and the city's merchants jockeyed to provision the hungry logging camps.

In 1851, James Welch began building what was likely the first sawmill in Astoria proper. A few years later the plant was purchased by the Parker brothers, Wilder and Hiram, who had a tradition of sawdust in their Vermont blood. Other pioneer sawmills rose across the Astoria area from Tongue Point to the shores of Youngs Bay. Ferdinand Ferrell soon became interested in the town's sawmills, and in 1861 built one of his own at 14th and Exchange Street, which was then along the waterfront.

Logs for these early mills came from no further away than the John Day and Walluski Rivers. The trees along the shore were simply felled into the water and cut into logs as they floated. Downed timber farther up the bank was coaxed into the drink using hand-powered ratcheting jacks. Once afloat, the logs were formed into a raft and towed to a

Built by Marshall J. Kinney in 1884, the Clatsop Mill was one of Astoria's leading sawmills in its time, cutting some 80,000 board feet of lumber per day. The mill site later became home to the Astoria Plywood Corporation, which operated until the 1990s. (CCHS 4.625)

nearby mill.

As the timberline receded beyond easy reach of tidewater, loggers yoked teams of oxen together and dragged the logs out of the forest over skidroads. The skidroad was little more than a suitably flat path across which small logs were placed every eight or 10 feet. These logs, or skids, were secured in the roadbed and hewed in the center to create a trough in which the logs would ride. Ox teams—as many as ten yokes, or 20 animals—would be led into the forest and shackled to a group of logs that had been maneuvered onto the skidroad and chained end-to-end. With the logs hooked to the team, the teamster, or "bullwhacker," commenced to drive the team slowly but steadily towards the rollway.

By the early 1880s, Astoria had three sawmills, all working feverishly just to keep up with local demand: lumber for buildings, planks for streets, timbers for ships, and tens of thousands of boxes

With a "turn" of logs chained to five yoke of oxen, the "bull whacker" stands at the ready to drive the team to tidewater. The bulls dragged the logs over "skidroads," which prevented them from becoming mired in the soil. (CCHS 685.615)

for canned salmon. At the same time, Leinenwever & Co. in Uppertown was extracting the tannin from hemlock bark to produce great quantities of leather goods. Across the river at Knappton, Captain Asa M. Simpson's big and busy steam sawmill was cutting shiploads of lumber for the Pacific trade.

With the increased demand for logs in Astoria and elsewhere along the river, loggers began to experiment with new-fangled steam-powered machines that promised to increase production. One of the trailblazing steam loggers in Clatsop County was John C. Trullinger, owner of Astoria's West Shore Mills. In 1884, he punched a railroad into a stand of timber along the Walluski River and commenced logging. He also bought a donkey engine patented only a few years before by California lumberjack John Dolbeer.

Steam-powered machinery would not oust the

last ox team until the early 1900s. By the outbreak of World War I, high-lead logging had become the new standard. In a tall spar tree, fastened securely to surrounding stumps by guy wires, huge pulleys or blocks were hung and steel cables ran out from the donkey, through the blocks, to the downed timber. Short noose-like chokers attached to one of these cables were fastened to the logs, the donkey engineer was given a signal, and the logs were yarded in, suspended over obstacles of all sorts. At the spar, the logs were loaded onto waiting railroad cars and brought out of the hills where they were dumped into tidewater and towed to the sawmill.

The 1920s and 1930s have come to be known as the "high-ball" logging era. Steam-powered machinery was at its zenith, the pace of work was fast, and the dangers many. It was a time marked by big camps and big crews. Sprawling railroad

networks like the Astoria Southern and Kerry Line reached dozens of miles into the timbered heartland of Clatsop County. Some have called this the "Glory Days of Logging," though with colossal production came enormous waste, both in forest resources and human lives.

By the outbreak of the Second World War, internal combustion engines had displaced much of the older technologies. Log trucks replaced costly logging railroads, while bulldozers and diesel-powered yarders sent steam donkeys to the scrap yard. The felling of trees by ax and cross-cut saw was done away with in favor of the chainsaw. This more mobile equipment gave rise to numerous small contract-logging firms, sometimes referred to as "gyppo" loggers. As forest roads improved, loggers abandoned the last of their Clatsop County logging camps in the 1940s and settled into the more domesticated confines of

Sorensen Logging Company's Climax locomotive pauses on the rails near Svenson, circa 1905. (CCHS 31.605)

Until around the time of the Second World War, the principle means of downing Clatsop County's giant trees was with rudimentary tools—axes and crosscut saws. (CCHS 53.620)

nearby towns.

Logging technology was not the only aspect of the industry to evolve during the 1940s. Conventional lumber became less important as a diversified forest products industry emerged, which featured paper and plywood and scores of other uses for wood fiber. The pioneer pulp mill in the Astoria area dates back to 1884, when the waters of Young River falls were harnessed to power a wood grinder. This plant eventually ended up in the hands of a corporate predecessor to Crown Zellerbach, a San Francisco-based firm that in the 1960s built an industry-leading pulp and paper mill at Wauna in northeastern Clatsop County. In the realm of plywood, the Astoria Plywood Corporation, a co-operative launched in the late 1940s, churned out veneer until the 1990s. Today, Mill Pond Village stands on the site.

The notion of re-growing commercial grade trees also took root around the time of the Second World War. Companies like Crown Zellerbach, which owned over 130,000 acres in Clatsop County, hired university-trained foresters to see that its timberlands remained productive. "Tree Farms" based on the evolving science of "sustained yield forestry" sought to bring order and predictability to all levels of an otherwise chaotic and seemingly wasteful natural order. With the desired forest structure—a balance of tree ages across the landscape—trees could be farmed like any other crop. This predictability promised a perpetual supply of wood products, stable high-paying jobs, and confidence for investors in forest-based enterprises.

Crown Zellerbach's plans for permanence were cut short in 1985 when corporate raider Sir James

Goldsmith took control of the company in a hostile takeover. Hundreds of loggers and mill workers were displaced as Goldsmith divided Crown's assets and, in the process, broke the local union representing the woods workers. Crown's Clatsop Managed Forest has traded hands several times since the takeover, but the industrial and state managed forests of Clatsop County still provide numerous jobs both in the logging industry and in the local mills.

Read More…

In the annals of Clatsop County logging history, two of the books that stand out are Sam Churchill's Big Sam and its sequel Don't Call Me Ma, both published by Doubleday & Company, in 1965 and 1977, respectively. In them, Churchill recounts stories of his logger-father "Big" Sam Churchill and his youthful years in the Western Cooperage logging camp 15 miles south of Astoria.

A Railroad to the Coast

The citizens of Astoria had great cause to celebrate on the third day of April 1898. After nearly a half-century of failed attempts, the last spike was finally driven on a rail line connecting their city to the outside world. The events leading up to this day had required extraordinary effort and sacrifice on the part of the Astorians. "As an example of self-dependence and public achievement," wrote historian Leslie M. Scott, "the completion of this railroad deserves to go down in the annals of things highly praiseworthy in Oregon."

Talk of a transcontinental rail link running down the Columbia River basin and all the way to the river's mouth began to circulate with the first railroad surveys of the 1850s. For several decades to follow, Astoria always came up in railroad development plans, but little ever materialized. In 1870, Congress proffered considerable land grants as incentive to build a railroad linking Portland with McMinnville and Astoria. The Oregon &

One of the headaches for train crews on the A. & C.R. were the several draw bridges located east of Astoria. Here a flagman awaits a train's crossing. (CCHS 3981.235)

The majority of the Astoria & Columbia River Railroad's passenger traffic consisted of Portland residents headed to and from the seashore on trains like this one, shown here near Seaside around 1910. During the railroad's heyday, two regular passenger trains made the round trip daily. (CCHS 406-235)

California Railroad, under the shrewd command of Ben Holladay, Oregon's first Railroad Baron, took much of the land but neglected to extend its rails coastward.

Holladay's successor, Henry Villard, did little to further Astoria's cause. An astute businessman, Villard believed that his monopolistic line of steamships flying the Oregon Railroad & Navigation Company flag could carry freight and passengers more efficiently than a railroad paralleling the lower Columbia. In 1881, Villard took control of the Northern Pacific Railroad, and two years later oversaw its completion, linking the Great Lakes with Portland and Puget Sound. The citizens of Clatsop County entreated Villard to push the rails downriver, but facing dwindling resources and prohibitive building costs, the Northern Pacific came only as far as Goble, nearly 60 miles shy of Astoria.

Hoping to force the railroad builders into action, Astorians petitioned Congress to repeal the unused Oregon & California land grants. In 1885 the repeal became law, and backfired terribly on its instigators. Rather than prompting the railroad to connect with Astoria, thereby saving its land

Passengers and onlookers throng the Astoria Railroad Depot, built in 1897. (CCHS 4325.235)

line had reached Seaside just as the company's finances began to falter. Reid tried to entice Collis P. Huntington, head of the Southern Pacific, to join the project but the deal fell through and work ceased. In 1892, another seemingly well-financed firm, The Astoria & Portland Railway, sent crews to work grading a similar route. Within months the funding dried up and this project too went to ruin.

Once again Astorians looked upriver for their rail connection. They stockpiled a considerable subsidy in both land and cash and sent invitations to would-be railroad builders. Promoters from New York, Utah, and even Europe arrived in Astoria to collect the bounty. Their schemes all faded.

A seven-car passenger train steams west across the long trestle linking Tongue Point with Astoria in about 1900. (CCHS 1116.235)

TONGUE POINT & COLUMBIA RIVER.
ASTORIA. OREG.
261.

grant, Villard and his successors chose not to act, leaving the city without government aid in developing the line. The citizens of Astoria would have to do it themselves.

Many boosters believed a line linking Clatsop County with the Tualatin Plains through the Nehalem country was the most practicable route. In 1889, the Astoria & South Coast Railway, under the direction of its principle investor, William Reid, began work on a line between Youngs Bay and Hillsboro. By the summer of 1890, the

Then, in 1894, Andrew B. Hammond arrived in town. He had come to Oregon from Montana to buy a bankrupt railroad, and stopped in Astoria out of curiosity. Originally from Quebec, Hammond had made considerable money under the Big Sky milling railroad ties and laying tracks, and soon found himself engaged to build Astoria's long-awaited railroad. Work on the line commenced in August 1895, and the Astoria & Columbia River Railroad was completed in April 1898. Hammond also bought the line between Seaside and Skipanon, and in 1896 brought its rails to Astoria over an 8,000-foot-long wooden trestle spanning Youngs Bay.

In 1907, Hammond sold the Astoria line to James J. Hill, owner of the Great Northern. Less than ten years later, the final link in the Columbia River Highway reached Astoria. At the time, few could have imagined that this crude highway and others to follow would make the railroad to the coast obsolete. The first sure sign of this came in 1957, the year passenger service was discontinued. Four decades more elapsed before freight traffic from Astoria came to an end.

The Astoria Line had been part of the Burlington Northern network since 1970, and in 1997 the Wyoming-based Portland & Western bought the section between the Rose City and Tongue Point. The trestles and tracks west of that became property of the City of Astoria. From 2003 to 2005, amid the hoopla over the Corps of Discovery's bicentennial, the old Astoria & Columbia River Railroad had a brief revival as a passenger line with the successful Lewis & Clark Explorer train that ran between Linnton and Astoria.

Life in the City

Cigar shop owner Dell Scully
fishes through cracks in Astoria's
streets in 1905. (CCHS 874.147)

The City on a Hill

Travel writers who visit Astoria often draw parallels between its terraced hillsides and stately homes to those of San Francisco. The comparison is a fair one, albeit on a different scale. In both localities the grandeur of the homes reflected the material wealth of its citizens, and in Astoria many of the most ornate dwellings can be traced back to the 1880s. It was the Victorian Era, a prim and proper time when such displays of extravagance were looked upon as monuments of refinement and symbols of Astoria's cosmopolitan future.

If the town were to grow into a great city, it would require an infrastructure to match. In 1884, a telephone exchange was built, and the following year the first electricity-generating plant powered up; three years later, trolley service began, and in 1892 the streetcars were electrified; in 1895, the municipal water system was upgraded, a large reservoir built, and the waters of Bear Creek piped throughout the city. Progress was measured by such improvements.

Smaller upgrades too brought a sense of uniformity to the city, like the standardization of Astoria's street names in 1895. East-west avenues, which honored a mishmash of Indian chiefs, American diplomats, and evergreens, were renamed in alphabetical sequence, while the north-south streets were given numbers.

The Victorian Era also saw the emergence of culture in Astoria as its citizens worked to smooth the edges from its pioneer past. They established music, literary, and social societies. Churches, schools, and newspapers, were becoming an ever-increasing part in the lives of many. By 1893, a public library located in City Hall welcomed cerebral types, though the number of volumes was limited.

Rats!

Sanitation was a straightforward matter for Astorians of the Victorian Era. The town's waste—residential refuse, offal from canneries, horse

stable aggregate, slaughterhouse scraps, sawmill residue—was jettisoned into the river. Eventually, the tide carried most of it away. "The stench in Astoria…" recalled one citizen, "was something to behold in memory."

The decomposing waste beneath the stilted city drew vermin of all kinds, especially rats, which for decades plagued Astoria's business district. Virtually every waterfront establishment owned at least one dog trained to stifle the rodents. Foard & Stokes, the general merchandise firm at 15th and Commercial, had a notable rat catcher in "Jack the Scotchman," a hairy black-and-white terrier. Jack could dispatch a rat with such skill and show that his work became a popular diversion among some Astorians.

Several aspiring Pied Pipers appeared at Astoria's doorstep throughout the years, but the town's rat problem was not fully resolved until the construction of a seawall in 1914.

Her STORY

Astoria's history is usually framed as a masculine battle against the natural elements: man versus the river or sea or forest. While this perspective is certainly a compelling component of the story, it neglects the role that women played in shaping the town. Their labors as homemakers, housekeepers, midwives, waitresses, cannery workers, and the myriad other positions they filled have long been under-appreciated. The women who yearned for professional careers frequently found their options limited, though a number became teachers or nurses. A few broke from the social norms of the time to practice medicine and serve in politics.

One of Astoria's most celebrated figures was Dr. Bethenia Owens-Adair, the first female doctor in the Pacific Northwest. She arrived in Clatsop County as a toddler in 1843 and at age 13 entered into an unhappy marriage. Her son, George, arrived in 1856 and three years later she was granted a divorce. It was then that she decided to pursue education. For a time, Owens-Adair taught school and eventually became successful in the millinery trade. With her business proceeds she attended medical school in Philadelphia and attained a degree as a "bath doctor"—the highest certificate available to a women at the time. In 1880, she became an M.D. and practiced medicine on and off until her death in 1926 at age 85.

In the realm of politics, Clatsop County's women achieved some notable milestones. In 1912, when an ambitious school clerk in Warrenton named Clara "Callie" Munson was elected that town's mayor, she made headlines as the first woman mayor west of the Rocky Mountains. The year of Miss Munson's election stands as the first time in Oregon's history that women could vote in a municipal election, the culmination of decades of work by women's suffrage groups. Less than a decade later, Mary Kinney, one of Astoria's leading businesswomen, became one of the state's first female legislators. Her work in the state legislature led to her election as state senator in 1922.

Bethina Owens-Adair
(CCHS 5595.00A)

Read More…

Dr. Bethenia Owens-Adair's memoir, the self-titled Dr. Owens-Adair: Some of Her Life Experiences, is a wonderful insight to the plight of 19th century Oregon women. Also featured in the book are sketches of other prominent pioneers, both men and women, who Owens-Adair knew personally.

DOINGS ALONG
Astor Street

During Astoria's zenith as a salmon canning and sawmilling center, a sound drink could be obtained at any number of establishments along the town's lengthy waterfront. But it was a stretch of Astor Street—from about 4th to 9th—that earned distinction as "Swilltown," a freewheeling strip that catered to all the needs and desires of loggers, fishers, and seafarers.

Swilltown's origins can be traced to the fishing bonanza of the 1870s. The sizeable population of footloose fishermen that descended upon the Columbia River every spring brought with them a penchant for intemperance. For decades to come, Astor Street would be home to an assortment of burlesque theaters, saloons, gambling halls, and "hotels" that served as working quarters for the establishments' many hostesses. While salmon were in the river, these industries flourished. "During the fishing season," reported *The Oregonian* in 1882, "it is perhaps the most wicked place on earth for its population."

During these wide-open years at the close of the 19th century, Astoria reputably hosted more saloons per capita of population than any other town in Oregon. The

most elegant drinking emporium of them all was The Louvre, located in the heart of Swilltown. Opened in the 1890s by a studious-looking Finn named August Erickson, The Louvre was billed as a first class drinkery with good order where "everybody's rights" were "strictly observed." He eventually left Astoria and opened the legendary Erickson's Saloon on Portland's West Burnside which purportedly the housed the West's longest bar, measuring 684 linear feet and taking up almost an entire city block.

Above the street-level watering holes, many saloons housed what were politely deemed "female boardinghouses." A number of the "land ladies" who oversaw the stable of strumpets upstairs made small fortunes and became respected citizens. Some of Astoria's most prominent citizens were known to patronize these establishments, though for them discrete doorways allowed entry and exit from Bond Street, not Astor.

Also scattered around the waterfront were a number of sailors' boardinghouses. It was upon the proprietors of these hostels that the captains of windjammers sometimes relied to fill their crew before departing on long ocean voyages. Many seamen signed on willingly. Others, who were not necessarily sailors, were delivered to the ship by shanghaiers. Crimps, as the shanghaiers were known, would employ alcohol, drugs, trickery,

and even violence to nab the unwary. Through trap doors, crimps passed unsuspecting or unconscious men into Astoria's watery underworld, where a rowboat waited to ferry them to the ship. For each man supplied, desperate captains paid the crimps "blood money."

One of Astoria's leading crimps was a diminutive Irish woman named Bridget Grant. This gentle-faced boardinghouse proprietor arrived in town in 1876, and together with her son Peter, fared well collecting blood money. Her handiwork even earned her the unkind distinction of being called the "queen of the boarding-masters' fraternity." The Grants were certainly not alone. For a time, Astoria was the base of operations for Jim Turk, one of Portland's most notorious crimps. Jim Cook and Mickey "Fat" Woods, too, operated in Astoria. In 1881, this bold duo abducted sailors from the ship *Palmyra* and ransomed them back to her skipper for $40 apiece.

Despite waves of moral crusades, city officials did little to rid the town of the sinful element along Astor Street. It was simply too lucrative. In 1880, over one-third of Astoria's municipal income came from city-mandated liquor license fees. Swilltown's proceeds helped fund Astoria's streets, schools, and civic projects. Shang-

haiing, too, was often overlooked by a police force that was occasionally reminded, with a little sweetener, not to interfere with business. By the early 1900s, though, the town's civic values began show signs of change.

Astoria's shanghaiing days passed with the era of the tall ships, and not long afterwards prohibition came to Oregon. In 1919, the manufacture and sale of alcohol became illegal nationwide, but by then Swilltown had lost much of its color. Brothels would remain open along Astor Street until the Second World War, when military officials began extinguishing the red lights. What federal prohibition and countless moral crusades could not destroy, the Oregon State Highway Department wiped clean when it rerouted Highway 30 through town. During the street widening process, most of the historic buildings lining Astor Street were razed and the last reminders of Swilltown disappeared.

Today, this once notorious street only extends three blocks along Astoria's waterfront. With the comfortable distance of time, many Astorians have come to appreciate this most colorful, if lowbrow, side of their history. Shanghaiing

returned to Astoria once again in 1984 when the Astor Street Opry Company premiered its melodrama "Shanghaied in Astoria." Set in 1904 and bursting with local color, the play, which has run every year since from July through September, has become a signature piece of contemporary Astorian culture.

Bridget Grant
(CCHS 5597.00G)

BREWED! in Astoria

In 1883, John Kopp arrived in Astoria and set up the North Pacific Brewing Company in Uppertown. His most recent brewing venture had been in Seattle where he had been a partner with Andrew Hemrich, who later became famous for producing a lager called "Rainier Beer." Though Kopp's handiwork never reached an international standing, for several decades it was the beverage of choice along the lower Columbia.

Commercial brewing had been a part of the Pacific Northwest for nearly three decades before Kopp came to Astoria. Thirsty Astorians had been contenting themselves with beer from Henry Wienhard and other Portland-area brewers until 1872, when Michael Myers opened the town's first brewery. The Columbia Brewery opened a few years later along Astor Street. By the 1880s, though, both operations had dried up.

The kettles and tubs from the Columbia Brewery were soon at work producing beer for the St. Louis Brewery along 17th Street. An interesting sidelight about this operation was that one of its proprietors, Theresa O'Brien, was a rare woman in the male-dominated brewing world of the 19th century. This firm ran its last batch in 1895.

By then, however, Bräumeister Kopp was Astoria's undisputed beer-making king, producing hundreds of barrels per month. As demand ex-

panded, so did Kopp's operation. In 1896, he built a modern brewing facility at 30th and Franklin that was the most expensive building ever put up in town to that time. His brewers were soon rolling out 200 barrels of beer per day.

In 1902, Kopp sold the North Pacific Brewing Company to his head brewer and other businessmen, who soon opened a branch brewery in Portland. The firm carried on a brisk business until 1915, when statewide prohibition made Oregon dry. In 1928, part of the brewery was remodeled into the Uppertown Fire Station, and since 1989 has served as the Clatsop County Historical Society's Firefighters Museum.

For nearly eight decades, commercial brewing was absent from Astoria. But after the long drought, in the early 1990s beer was once again brewed in the river city, albeit in relatively small quantities. This resurgence in beer making grew out of the "craft beer" movement that has established the Pacific Northwest as the uncontested microbrewery capital of the country. In recent years, Astoria has become home to skillful and innovative brewers who have earned a reputation for producing outstanding craft beer. John Kopp would no doubt be proud.

ASTORIA EVENING BUDGET

United Press Telegraphic News Service.

Contains all the Local News Fit to Print

...TORIA EVENING BUDGET   ASTORIA, OREGON,   MONDAY, MARCH 3, 1919.   SIX PAGES   PRICE FIVE CENTS

THE WEATHER

MEDFORD MAYOR UNDER ARREST

GERMANY TRIES

DISARMAMENT IS UNDER DISCUSSION

MATTER BEING CONSIDERED BY THE SUPREME WAR COUNCIL

AMERICANS AT BERLIN TARGET

Astorian Evening Budget

WESTWARD THE COURSE OF EMPIRE TAKES ITS WAY

THE MORNING ASTORIAN (1873) AND ASTORIA BUDGET (1892) CONSOLIDATED

ASTORIA, OREGON, TUESDAY, FEBRUARY 4, 1941

Sees Aid Bill Leading U.S. Into War

British

From *The Western American* to the Finnish *Toveri*

The Story of Astoria's Newspapers

A great deal of Astoria's history can be gathered through an examination of its newspapers. Not a page-by-page shuffle though yellowed broadsheets or endless rolls of eye-bending microfilm—though that too is a worthwhile exercise—but rather an inspection of the newspapers' titles, publication dates, frequency, and its editor's rallying points. Local papers, after all, depend on the local audience and advertisers, often making its tone as noteworthy as the news they carried.

The town's first paper, for example, was named the *Marine Gazette*. Initially published in 1864 at the insistence of local promoters, the title suggests the would-be city's interest at the time. It was waterborne trade, in fact, that brought the *Gazette*'s second owner to Astoria, when in 1861, William L. Adams and family arrived to fill his new post as customs collector. Adams, together with his son-in-law W. W. Parker, took over the paper, but by 1866 the *Marine Gazette* had sunk.

Astoria's second newspaper, the *Astorian*, had more staying power, at 138 years and counting. It began as a weekly, but as the town's fishing fortunes ballooned, it blossomed into a daily three years later. That was in 1876, and the following year its publisher, DeWitt Clinton Ireland, installed a steam engine to operate his busy press. Ireland was among the most colorful of Oregon's frontier newspapermen. He was known to be a hard drinker who consorted with the town's seamier residents and, it was said, unafraid to flex his editorial pen for the right price.

In 1881, P.W. Parker and Joseph Halloran purchased the *Astorian* from Ireland. Under their partnership, the *Astorian* became known for its excellent writers and cutting edge equipment. In 1892, for example, Parker and Halloran brought the first linotype machine to Oregon.

With the town's rapid growth during the 1880s came a flood of aspiring publications. The new weeklies included the *Columbia*, the *Gateway-Herald*, the *Press*, the *Express*, the *Evening Bulletin*, the *Examiner*, as well as the sporadically published *Eagle* and *Town Talk*. One weekly that survived longer than most was O. W. Dunbar's *Evening Budget*, which first rolled off the press in 1892.

Reflecting the town's influx of immigrants, by the 1880s Astoria had both Swedish-language and Finnish-language newspapers. Others fol-

lowed. In 1907, the *Toveri*, a bi-weekly publication of the Finnish Socialist Federation, was first printed in Astoria. The *Toveri* became a daily in 1912 and, due to its regional aim, could soon boast of a circulation greater than all of Astoria's English-language newspapers combined. The paper grew increasingly leftist until it ceased publication in 1931. More moderate newspapers were printed at least partially in Finn until the 1950s.

In 1919, Edwin Aldrich, Fred Lampkin, and Lee Drake, owners of Pendleton's *East Oregonian*, bought the *Astoria Evening Budget* and appointed one of their most promising staff writers to be its editor. His name was Merle Chessman. From the *Evening Budget*'s editorial page, Chessman railed against corruption in his newly adopted home, which led to a new city charter that included the position of city manager. Another of his battles was with the Ku Klux Klan in its effort to fill local government with Klan members. This fight Chessman ultimately lost.

The Klan was a powerful force in Astoria of the 1920s. At its height, the local Klavern had some 2,000 members, unified by their opposition to Catholics, Communists, and immigrants. Editor Chessman's criticism of the group led to several boycotts against the *Evening Budget* and even an offer from the Klan to buy the paper. For a time, Imperial Klansman Lem A. Dever even published *The Western American*, the Ku Klux Klan's West Coast newspaper, from Astoria.

Astoria's K.K.K. days ended by 1928, but Merle Chessman's estimable career as editor and publisher would continue through the Second World War. The Great Depression hit Astoria hard, and as the city's population began to shrink, it could no longer support two dailies. In 1930, the *Astoria Evening Budget* and the *Astorian* were merged to create the *Astorian Budget*. The streamlined *Astorian Budget* continued to push for civic improvements such a bridge spanning the Columbia River and a naval base at Tongue Point. After Chessman's untimely death in 1947, his son Robert took over the job until leaving the *Astorian* in 1960.

In the meantime, J. W. "Bud" Forrester and his wife, Eleanor, who was the daughter of Edwin Aldrich, became financially involved in the East Oregonian Publishing Company. In 1973, the Forresters moved to Astoria where Bud took the position of editor at *The Daily Astorian*. Fourteen years later, Bud and Eleanor's son, Steve, succeeded his father as editor, a position he still holds as Astoria celebrates its bicentennial.

Bethania Norwegian Lutheran Church along Franklin Street in Uppertown. (CCHS 33844.520)

Houses *of* Worship

Astoria's historic reputation as a den of debauchery and vice often overshadows its deep-rooted ecclesiastical side. As Christian doctrine came west with missionaries and early pioneers, the importance of church life grew as the town swelled with God-fearing European immigrants in the late 1800s. Evidence of this Christian tradition can be seen in the numerous steeples rising from the cityscape. Inside these sanctuaries it is not unusual for multiple generations of families to belong to the same congregation.

Clatsop Plains was an early hotbed of Christian fervor. To this expanse of grassland south of the Columbia River's mouth came missionaries from the Methodist Church as part of Jason Lee's "Great Reinforcement." In 1840, they built a mission from logs and set about spreading the gospel. With songs and services performed in Chinook Jargon—a hybrid trade language composed mostly of English, French, and Chinook words—the evangelists labored to convert the Plains' indigenous population, though the exact number of souls saved by the missionaries is not of record.

Methodism was not the only theological stirring on Clatsop Plains during that period. In the fall of 1846, Plains residents organized the first Presbyterian Church west of the Rocky Mountains. The congregation met in one another's homes until 1850 when they built a church on land donated by Robert and Nancy Morrison. In 1872 another wooden structure replaced the original church, and in 1927 the brick Gray Memorial Chapel was erected and named for William and Mary Gray, early missionary-settlers.

The 1840s also witnessed the first Methodist meetings in Astoria proper. James Welch donated a plot of land near what is now 15th and Franklin so that the congregants would have a place to gather. In 1853, they erected the Methodist Episcopal Church, the first house of worship in Astoria. Today their church building is at 11th and Franklin. Those of the Episcopalian persuasion organized in 1864, followed in 1877 by the Presbyterians, and in 1878 by the Baptists. Like the Methodists, the Episcopalians (Grace Episcopal), Presbyterians (First Presbyterian), and Baptists (First Baptist) still conduct regular services in Astoria.

Astoria's Roman Catholic congregation dates to shortly after the Civil War, when Father Patrick Gibney organized the parish and oversaw the building of an abbey. A group of soldiers stationed at Fort Stevens aided the clergyman in his efforts,

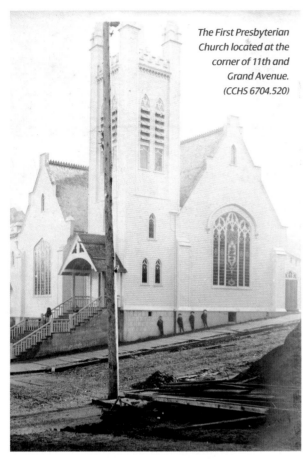

performing much of the physical work as well as becoming charter members. The church became St. Mary's Star of the Sea, which in 1902 moved into a new building on the 1400 block of Grand Avenue. In addition to Catholic services, St. Mary's has long maintained a parish school and, before its closure in 1971, operated an affiliated hospital and nursing program.

In the 1870s, adherents of Lutheranism began to convene in Astoria. As the predominant Protestant tradition in northern Europe, the number of Lutheran churches mirrors the influx of Scandinavian and German immigrants to Asto-

ria. Germans and Norwegians were the first to establish Lutheran worship services, followed by the Swedes and Finns. In many of these churches, services were conducted in the native language of its organizers, which in some instances continued well into the 20th century.

The Rev. Peter Carlson organized the Swedish Lutheran Church in Uppertown in 1880, and for a time held services in the nearby Scandinavian-American Cannery. The congregation soon built a church along Franklin Avenue near 33rd Street. Around 1908, the Swedish-based Memorial Lutheran Church began offering services in English. Memorial Lutheran attracted both American-born Scandinavians as well as Astoria's German Lutherans who had been without a church of their own for some time. In 1929, First Swedish and Memorial Lutheran were combined to form Trinity Lutheran Church.

In 1883, the Finnish Evangelical Lutheran Church came into existence under the guidance of Pastor J. J. Hoikka. The multilingual Hoikka could deliver sermons in Swedish, Finnish, or English and, on occasion, was called upon to do so for other congregations. The more conservative Finnish Apostolic Lutheran Church dates to this period, as does the Finnish Congregational Church. In 1974, the Finnish Lutheran Church, then known as Zion Lutheran, merged with Trinity Lutheran to create Peace Evangelical Lutheran Church.

During the early decades of the 1900s, other houses of worship were organized in Astoria, including those of the Assembly of God, Jehovah's Witnesses, Bible Baptists, and Seventh Day Adventists. Also among these newer congregations was The Church of Jesus Christ of Latter-Day

Saints, which began with 17 members in 1936. That year, there were 19 different churches in the city.

Although Christianity has been the predominant religion in Astoria, it has not been alone. The town long had a small Jewish community—its early members were almost exclusively of German extraction—but it was not until around the Second World War that a synagogue was formed. The Beth Israel Congregation, at 13th and Grand Avenue, served a small following and was never able to support a resident rabbi. Still, for special occasions and Jewish holidays, the faithful would assemble for rites.

Christianity of one persuasion or another remains the city's leading faith. Today there are some 25 houses of worship within the city limits, and though each has a unique story, they all stand as an ever-present reminder of Astoria's ongoing religious tradition.

Astoria's First Evangelical Lutheran Church. (CCHS 23023.530)

schools

On October 27, 1957, a crowd gathered to celebrate the dedication of Astoria's new high school located near the banks of Youngs Bay. It was a thoroughly modern facility, costing nearly two million dollars, and capable of accommodating 900 students. At the time, public education in Astoria was already a century old, and its evolution reflected both the growth of the city as well as its broadening social values.

A two-room shack belonging to Conrad Boel-ling provided Astoria's first schoolhouse. That was in 1851. The school's 10 or so pupils received instruction in the front room from teacher Chauncey Hosford who made his living quarters in the rear chamber. Three years later, School District Number One was organized. Few of Astoria's buildings were available for or equipped to handle large groups of children, so the Methodist Church housed the district's classes.

In 1859, the first public school was built near what is today 9th and Exchange Streets. It too was a modest affair, but it afforded class space for kindergarten through high school age students. In 1864, the district dropped its high school program when Grace Episcopal Church opened its parish school and began offering secondary studies. A decade later, a school opened in Uppertown and operated as its own district until 1892.

To accommodate Astoria's growing population in the 1880s and 1890s, several new school buildings were erected, each named for the historic district in which it stood. In 1882, the Shively School at 16th and Exchange opened; a year later the McClure School at 7th and Grand; the Alderbrook School began accepting students in 1892; and the Taylor School in Uniontown a decade later.

In 1890, a handful of high school students began attending classes on the top floor of the McClure School. The first class of Astoria High School graduates—all three of them—received their diplomas in 1893. For most youths of the period, formal schooling ended after the eighth grade, as economic necessity compelled them find work to help support their families. That began to change in the early 1900s, however, as more teenagers had the opportunity to pursue secondary school. As enrollment grew, a high school was built upon the hill at 16th and Jerome in 1911.

For nearly a half-century, the high school at the top of 16th Street was home to grades 10 through 12. The last class of graduating seniors passed through the doors of the building in 1957, when the new high school opened. The following year, the old high school—and its Patriot Hall annex, built in the early 1920s—became Clatsop Community College, which still serves as a place of enlightenment and enrichment for residents of Astoria and the surrounding communities.

Since 1905, the *Zephyrus*, the high school's

High School, Astoria, Oreg.

The McClure School, circa 1904. The upper story of this building served as Astoria High School from 1890 until 1911. (CCHS 4272.503)

yearbook, has tracked Astoria's students and their activities. According to Bruce Berney, who painstakingly indexed nearly a century's worth of annuals, the *Zephyrus* evolved from a literary journal begun by students in 1894 called the *High School Quill*. Zephyrus, it is worth noting, is the Greek god of the west wind, which in Astoria is an elemental force.

The early decades of the 1900s saw the old wooden elementary schools replaced by masonry structures. The first was Central School in 1917, so named for its relative location. Then came the Robert Gray School, built in 1924, which served the children of Astoria's west end. A year later in Uppertown, the John Jacob Astor School opened.

More recent additions to the school district have been a middle school on Astoria's south slope and the Lewis & Clark Elementary School across Youngs Bay.

There is much to be proud of and hopeful about as Astoria's school system enters its 16th decade. Over the years school buildings have come and gone, as have teachers and students, but one thing remains constant: the community's long-standing support of public education.

Astoria's FIRES

July 2, 1883 and December 8, 1922

The Uppertown Fire Station No. 2, seen here in 1930, served the community from the 1920s until the 1960s. Originally built as a beer storage facility for the North Pacific Brewery, the building is now home to the Clatsop County Historical Society's Uppertown Firefighters Museum. (CCHS 3343.734)

Fire on the *Waterfront*

July 2, 1883

The year 1883 opened as one of the finest in Astoria's history. The town's thirty canneries were on pace to pack more salmon than ever before. The three big waterfront sawmills were busy cutting lumber at a phenomenal rate. Business was humming.

But on the evening of July 2, 1883, a fire started in the tinderbox of dry sawdust under "Dad" Ferrell's sawmill in the center of Astoria's waterfront. The plant at 14th and Exchange Streets was a roiling sheet of flames in minutes. The conflagration spread to the mill's box factory and storage sheds before the volunteer fire department could even get their pumpers into position.

Storeowners hitched up wagons and began to shuttle their goods away from the encroaching inferno. Volunteers lent a hand as well, hustling furniture from hotels, merchandise from stores, liquor from saloons, and whatever else could be carried to safety. Amid the chaos the wares were simply piled in nearby streets.

The fire ate through businesses lining Commercial Street as it fanned out toward the waterfront. As evening approached, the fire spread to the expansive Oregon Railway & Navigation dock where thousands of cases of canned salmon were neatly stacked for shipment. As the canned juices came to a boil the tin canisters exploded, exposing the fatty meat within that smoldered in a smoky heap. The sound of bursting cans could be heard all night and through much of the following day.

Miraculously, St. Mary's Hospital at 15th and Exchange was saved by bucket brigades that spread soaked bed covers over the roof. Other buildings were not so lucky as the destruction continued along the waterfront all the way to 17th Street. Crews labored to control the blaze, and with the aid of a pump boat spraying from the river were able to do so after nightfall.

That night as the red glow of flaming rubble lit the streets, Astoria's lower element helped themselves to the unattended casks of liquor. Soon, rescued goods lying in the street were being pilfered and looters began breaking into unscathed storefronts. Shop owners and local police officers tried to guard the heaps of goods, but to little avail. By sunrise the fire had run its course but the thievery continued.

The following day a vigilance committee was formed to recover the stolen merchandise. Headed by Isaiah Case, one of Astoria's leading

dirty work behind them, the citizens of Astoria commenced observing the most somber Fourth of July in the town's history.

Rebuilding began at once. Thanks to proceeds from a salmon pack that would prove to be the greatest on record, work progressed quickly. Astoria's lone remaining sawmill, John C. Trullinger's West Shore Mills, worked day and night to churn out lumber for the ambitious project. Whether it was due to the haste of rebuilding or the economics of it, Astorians repeated the all-wood design in their new waterfront that would make the city a time bomb for the next catastrophic blaze that sparked in 1922.

businessmen, the committee issued a proclamation demanding all stolen items be returned to City Hall. It went unnoticed. So, with the blessing of local authorities, the citizen's committee took action. The next night, one of the known leaders of the thieving horde was taken to the cemetery after a short hearing and given a choice: hanging or whipping. A rope was very deliberately thrown over a large limb in a nearby tree, and not far off a freshly dug grave was plainly visible. The lawbreaker quickly opted for the lashings and the next morning gladly accepted passage on a Portland-bound steamboat. The following evening, the vigilance committee gave another thug the same option. Lashes once again. City Hall was soon inundated with returned merchandise.

A new proclamation was issued to the remaining rabble-rousers that read: "Astoria, July 4th, 1883, To -----, you are hereby notified to leave Astoria, within 24 hours, not to return. Signed Citizen's Committee." The targeted hoodlums hurriedly left town, while others skedaddled without so much as an invitation to do so. With the

the
GREAT
FIRE

December 8, 1922

weinhard Hotel, Astoria Nat Bank
After Fire Woodfield Photo

It had been nearly four decades since the "Great Fire" ravaged Astoria. Those who had been there vividly recalled the event, but to a newer generation of Astorians it was little more than the subject of old-timers' tales. Then, on a raw winter morning in 1922, an even greater fire would level nearly the entire downtown district in one of the worst civic conflagrations in Pacific Northwest history. The only thing more remarkable than the thoroughness of the city's devastation was its citizens' faith, determination, and vision when it came time to rebuild.

At a quarter past two in the morning, alarms rang out alerting the fire department that smoke was billowing from the Beehive Department Store near 12th and Commercial Streets. Firemen from the nearby station reached the scene in minutes. When they opened a trap door to the adjacent Thiel Brothers Pool Hall, a great surge of flames swept the helmets from their heads. It was as if Hell itself had breached the surface.

Fire Chief Charles E. Foster ordered water on the fire as reinforcements arrived from Astoria's other stations. The lighthouse tender *Manzanita* was summoned and began to get up steam to pump from the river, though the fire was still some distance from the waterfront. Volunteers from the gathering crowd lent a hand in the effort, though the increasing throng of onlookers soon became a hindrance to the firefighters.

As crews doused the inferno, buildings on the opposite side of Commercial burst into flames. Then the water main under Commercial Street that fed the firemen's hoses melted and ruptured. The spray from the hoses fell to a trickle. A pumper crew hurriedly moved their engine and began to draft out of the river. In the meantime, and unbeknownst to Chief Foster, a truck full of loggers was bringing a load of dynamite to the scene to blow fire breaks around the growing blaze.

The situation continued to deteriorate. As the flames fanned out from Commercial Street the power went out and gas mains ruptured. In the chaotic scramble to save goods from threatened shops, law-abiding citizens and looters alike rushed through the smoke-filled streets with arms full of merchandise. The thunderous booms of the loggers' dynamite joined the gasoline-charged explosions of doomed filling stations to punctuate the roar of the fire.

Astoria Mayor James Bremner called for assistance from Portland, but by then the fire was in control. The plush Weinhard-Astoria Hotel was engulfed, and then the Astoria National Bank. By now, spray from the *Manzanita's* hoses could easily reach the flames that enveloped the waterfront on the fire's north side. The conflagration leapt from building to building, entering masonry structures through shattered windows, and leveling everything in its path. When the fire abated around noontime, some 32 blocks had been reduced to a rubble-strewn, ashy desert.

A light snow began to fall as Astorians took stock of their gutted city. Three people had died—one by suicide, one by drowning, and another, a car dealer, of a heart attack while pushing automobiles from his lot. Estimates placed the property damage in excess of $11 million. Hundreds were left homeless. Over 220 businesses had been destroyed, most of which were not covered by insurance due to the high premiums that providers required for the old wooden city.

Astoria had been built to burn, and Chief Foster knew it. According to historian Walter Mattila, the venerable fire chief had long protested the city's haphazard building codes and the placing of water mains on wooden viaducts beneath the streets. Foster's concerns were well-founded, as the viaducts acted as huge bellows to fan the flames and provided combustible material to carry the fire from block to block. As the water mains burned and broke, there was little water pressure to battle the fire.

But the ingredients for such a catastrophic fire predate Foster's tenure as head of the department. During the 1870s and 1880s, when Astoria was experiencing rapid growth, the downtown area was simply thrown up. Frame buildings were constructed atop piling, as were the streets. Everything was connected by wood. In the ensuing years, sand was pumped under portions of downtown, but all of the structures were still linked by wooden viaducts, and in places, timber-planked streets. Essentially, "The Great Fire of 1922" wiped out everything in downtown that had been built on piling.

Around the time of the fire, Astoria's municipal government was undergoing a metamorphosis that would prove beneficial to the city's rebuilding effort. The old city council form of government was done away with in favor of a city manager system. The move had been prompted by the city's deplorable financial condition and a tradition of graft associated with the previous administrative structure. Astoria's first city manager, and the one tasked with overseeing the rebuilding the city, was O. A. Kratz.

Funding the reconstruction work proved to be a tricky matter. Federal disaster relief was essentially unheard of at the time, and some outside of

For decades, Astoria's streets were built of Douglas fir timbers and planks. This crew is building such a street, which provided the fire a fuel sources as it spread from block to block in December 1922. (CCHS 7756.910)

Astoria doubted the city's ability to rebound from the catastrophe at all. Complicating the issue was the bonded indebtedness that hung over the city from its part in developing the Port of Astoria less than a decade before. Now, with its business district leveled, the situation looked grim. But the Astorians pulled together to forestall bankruptcy and soon had a plan to retire the debt and fund the rebuilding.

City Manager Kratz, an advisory panel called The Committee of Ten, and Astoria's selfless business community began to remake the city at once. The work commenced in two stages. First,

the public works projects of installing streets, sidewalks, sewers, water, and lights had to be completed before private enterprises could erect buildings. The streets were widened and, instead of being supported by wooden viaducts, were built up with concrete and filled with sand dredged from the river.

With a new street grid in place the private phase of reconstruction began. The property owners' faith in their city was evidenced by their re-investment in the burnt district. Scores of new concrete and brick buildings went up, including the eight-story Hotel Astoria, the Hotel Elliott, the Elks Temple, and the Sanborn Building. August Spexarth, who experienced the fire of 1883, built four new buildings and repaired a fifth in the fire's aftermath. To this day, Astoria's business district retains the look and feel of this era of rebirth, a legacy of "The Great Fire of 1922."

Cable Television

Astoria holds the title to many firsts, but one of the most surprising is that cable television originated on the rooftop of the Astoria Hotel in 1948. The previous year, Leroy "Ed" Parsons and his wife, Grace, were at a broadcasters' convention in Chicago where they saw television for the first time. Mrs. Parsons, so the story goes, began to hint that she wanted a TV. But Ed, being something of a genius with radio communications, knew that it would be impossible to pick up a television signal in Astoria—there were no broadcasting stations in the entire Pacific Northwest at the time.

A few months later, Parsons found out that a television station would be launched in Seattle in the fall of 1948. He went to work devising a way to receive the broadcast signal some 125 miles to the south. After a bit of tinkering, Ed placed an antenna atop the Astoria Hotel and strung a coaxial cable across the street to his apartment. When KRSC-TV hit the air on Thanksgiving Day, 1948, Ed and Grace Parsons were watching on their nine-inch black-and-white screen. It didn't take long for word of Ed's new apparatus to spread, and soon the Parsons' living room was full of people crowding around to catch a glimpse of the small screen.

Ed Parsons' hobby soon became a business. He set up more antennas, including one on Coxcomb Hill, built amplifiers, and threaded cables into his customers' homes. The system was a success. Ed and Grace left Astoria in 1953, but not before Ed started a radio station with the call letter KVAS.

Radio Waves

Astoria's KAST is Oregon's second oldest radio station. Listeners first tuned in back in 1922, when radio was little more than a novelty appreciated by the era's techies. The medium caught on in a big way, however, and around 1935 the 250-watt station became the area's first commercial radio station at 1370 on the AM dial. In the 1950s, KAST was joined by other long-lived radio stations, including KKEE in 1950 and KVAS two years later. Pat O'Day, the Seattle DJ sometimes called the "Godfather of Northwest Rock-N-Roll," got his first job in broadcasting at KVAS in 1956.

Coast Community Radio

For nearly three decades, the greater Astoria area has supported KMUN 91.9 FM, the local public radio station, which began broadcasting from the Gunderson Building in downtown in 1983. Five years later, the station moved into the Tillicum House, a spacious Craftsman home gifted to KMUN by Helen Patti. Today, KMUN is a National Public Radio member and maintains sister stations 89.5 KTCB Tillamook and 90.9 KCPB Warrenton, which are known collectively as Coast Community Radio.

Oregon, My Oregon

Not many Oregonians can recite the lyrics to their state song "Oregon, My Oregon." Even less well known than the recondite words of the anthem is the name of its originator, John Andrew Buchanan. Born in Iowa in 1863, Buchanan became a lawyer and was stationed at Fort Stevens during World War I. He fell in love with the area, and after the armistice moved his family to Astoria where he opened a law office in 1919. Buchanan became a civic leader and did a considerable amount of writing—penning "Oregon, My Oregon" in 1920—before he passed away in 1935.

In 1927, Buchanan's lyrics, set to music composed by Henry Bernard Murtagh, became Oregon's state song:

> Land of the Empire Builders,
> Land of the Golden West;
> Conquered and held by free men,
> Fairest and the best.
> Onward and upward ever,
> Forward and on, and on;
> Hail to thee, Land of Heroes,
> My Oregon.
>
> Land of the rose and sunshine
> Land of the summer's breeze;
> Laden with health and vigor,
> Fresh from the Western seas.
> Blest by the blood of martyrs,
> Land of the setting sun;
> Hail to thee, Land of Promise,
> My Oregon.

ASTORIA ATHLETICS

Walter "Wally" Palmberg holds a unique place in local sports history. In his youth he was an All-State standout on two of Astoria High School's state championship basketball teams. Wally then became an All-American at Oregon State University under Coach Amory "Slats" Gill, returning to Astoria as a teacher where he coached the Fighting Fishermen to two more state titles. Even with this impressive record, perhaps his most lasting contribution came a half-century later when he wrote the book *Toward One Flag: The Contribution of Lower Columbia Athletics, 1865-1943*.

The flag referred to in the title of Palmberg's book is not one found on an athletic field. It is the American flag. The tome's premise, and a mightily convincing one at that, focuses on the profound roll that team sports played in Americanizing foreign-born Astorians and unifying the community

as a whole. The entrenched divisions between Astoria's different nationalities—the product of centuries of Old World animosity—seemed to melt away in the sports arena. It was a lengthy and unplanned melding, but as Palmberg's book illustrates, team sports had the power to weave a new social fabric from Alderbrook to Uniontown and beyond.

Baseball was the earliest American team sport

to find a following in the Astoria area. The game came to Fort Stevens in 1865 with Civil War soldiers from back east, and for the next half-century hard ball would be a leading summer pastime in communities along the lower Columbia. Every backwater village that could assemble nine able bodies had a team, as did numerous logging camps and lumber mills. The squads formed leagues, made schedules, and converted nearby cow pastures into playable fields. Steamboats carried players and fans to away games, and after the contest, festive picnics allowed both sides to mingle.

From the 1890s until the early decades of the 1900s, athletic clubs were popular places for Astoria's youth to fraternize and compete. Membership consisted largely of teens who could not or chose not to attend high school, and club-organized events offered them a means to meet young people from enclaves beyond their own. The *Owa Pun Pun* Club, founded in Alderbrook in 1902, was one such organization. "Owa Pun Pun," its members insisted, was a Native American term that described West Astoria as a place of skunks. Great sports rivalries developed between Astoria's different neighborhoods—Alderbrook, Uppertown, Scow Bay, Downtown, Uniontown—that usually split along ethnic lines, though over the ensuing years those divisions began to blur.

Organized in Uppertown in 1910, Columbia Club counted among its members Norwegians, Swedes, Danes, Icelanders, Finns, Germans, Italians, and Greeks. Member Ted Jackson recalled, "though communication was sometimes at odds they all got along quite well…" Sports were the featured attraction, but only part of the schedule of events for the heterogeneous Columbia Club, which also included dances, banquets, concerts, and plays. These wholesome functions, carried out under the watchful eyes of the club's women's auxiliary, earned the organization a glowing reputation among parents and truancy officers alike.

Team sports took longer to catch on in the Finnish enclave of Uniontown. Though as a people they cherished athletics, particularly Old Country standards like wresting and track, to older Finns American team sports seemed, well, too American. Their offspring saw things differently. Under the banner of the loosely organized West Astoria Athletic Club, Uniontown's young men began competing in baseball, football, and basketball. In time, the Finns of Uniontown became as fanatical as any of Astoria's sports supporters.

By the 1920s, with more teenagers attending high school, the neighborhood athletic clubs gave way to one sports outlet representing the entire town: Astoria High School. No longer were participants playing for Uppertown or Uniontown, but their hometown. The ethnic divisions that remained mattered little when Astoria took the field or court against Salem, Oregon City, or one of the Portland high schools.

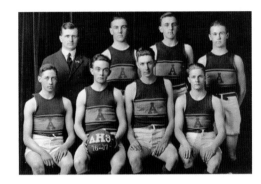

Basketball Town

Perhaps it's the weather that prompts Astoria's youth to excel at one particular indoor sport. Or, maybe it's something in the water. Whatever the reason, it's no secret among followers of Oregon prep athletics that Astoria is a basketball town.

After Oregon instituted its statewide high school basketball tournament in 1920, the Fighting Fishermen were regular attendees, missing only two tournaments between then and 1943. Though competing against every school in the state both large and small, six times during those years Astoria brought home the first place trophy. The first was in 1930. They brought the title home again in 1932, 1934, 1935, 1941, and 1942. When the University of Oregon won the first National Collegiate Athletic Association basketball tournament in 1939, five members of the legendary "Tall Firs" team were Astoria alumni.

One of the renowned names in Astoria athletics is that of Coach John Warren, who arrived in Astoria in the fall of 1928. Though widely remembered for his instruction on the gridiron—the high school football field bears his name—he first won acclaim as a basketball coach. His work off the court was equally commendable. Warren cared little about his players' ethnic heritages, and as he got to know them and their parents, his egalitarian attitude seemed to spread. Though his tenure at Astoria High School was relatively short, Warren set a standard that has been the measure for every coach since. He left A.H.S. after the 1935 school year to take a coaching position in the football program at his college alma mater in Eugene.

The high school fielded highly competitive teams—both boys and girls squads—through the second half of the century, but Astoria's next state basketball championship did not come until 1998. At the helm for the Fishermen was Coach Mike Goin. During his 24-year tenure as the head of the boys basketball program, Goin became the winningest coach in A.H.S. history, taking teams to the state tournament 17 times. Goin has since hung up his whistle, but a home game against local rivals Knappa or Seaside still packs in the crowd, a sure sign that Astoria's basketball legacy will last long into the future.

The Home Front
World War II Comes to Astoria

Soldiers from Fort Stevens examine a crater created by one of 17 artillery shells fired at the fort by a Japanese submarine on the night of June 21, 1942. (CCHS 2365.751)

Around noon on December 7, 1941, Astoria's regular Sunday radio programming was interrupted with a news bulletin informing listeners that Japanese forces had dealt the U.S. Navy a devastating blow with a surprise attack on Pearl Harbor. Additional details were sketchy, but many realized that Astoria would be a beachhead in the invasion of the Northwest Coast, if one were to come. Though defensive preparations had begun months before, the unease of that day would linger. For the next several years Astorians found themselves on the frontlines of the home front.

Living in a community with close links to trans-Pacific commerce, Astorians were well aware of the tensions that had been growing on the other side of the ocean during the late 1930s.

The town's Chinese population had agitated for embargos against Imperial Japan since at least 1938, but federal action was not taken until the fall of 1941. Out at Fort Stevens, Colonel Clifford Irwin had his 249th Coast Artillery practicing its marksmanship on an ever-increasing basis and his men on a rigid duty schedule. A Civilian Defense Council office had been established in Clatsop County, volunteers registered and, by the fall of 1941, observation posts were in place to monitor both the sea and sky.

The early stages of the war were a fast-paced time in Astoria. Troops and armaments poured in to town by the trainload. The military requisitioned an auto ferry, *Tourist No. 2*, renamed it *Octopus*, and used it to lay mines at the mouth of the Columbia River. Patrol planes buzzed overhead. From Naval Air Station Tongue Point—a base completed only shortly before the war—came PBY Catalina seaplanes. From Navy Scouting Squadron 50's hangar at the Astoria Airport, Kingfishers, Wildcats, and Seagulls took to the air. Volunteers scanned the skies from local mountaintops while beach patrols watched the waves for enemy submarines.

On the night of June 21, 1942, the war came to Astoria's doorstep when artillery shells began exploding around Fort Stevens. A foreign enemy had not bombarded a fortification in the continental United States since the War of 1812, but around 11:20 p.m., 17 rounds from a Japanese submarine whizzed over the skeleton of the *Peter Iredale* and landed just beyond in an open field. The guns at the fort were ordered not to return fire so as not to reveal their position. Though the shelling caused no damage, it was a potent wakeup call to local residents that the war was a very real matter.

Another unpleasant reminder of the wartime struggle involved the removal of the local Japanese community. A few months before Fort Stevens was attacked, some 60 Japanese residents of Clatsop County had been ushered onto buses at Astoria and taken to Portland under military convoy. Executive Order 9066, signed by President Franklin Roosevelt, made possible the removal of all persons of Japanese ancestry from the strategic West Coast defensive zone. Able to take only what they could carry, these unfortunate souls would spend the remainder of the war behind barbed wire at inland interment camps.

For most Astorians, though, the war years were marked by blackout and air raid drills, scrap drives, and ration books. Sacrifice was a burden shared by all. Tires and gas were hard to get, as were shoes and many basic foodstuffs. Nylon stockings, too, were unknown to a generation of girls who came of age during the war. Scrap drives for rags, paper, and metal became community events, as was the push to buy war bonds.

As the town filled with soldiers, sailors, flyboys, and Coasties, places like the Amato's Supper Club

Fleet Reserve - Astoria, Oregon

and Club 13 became happening spots. Dances and big band concerts offered a welcome diversion for many. One leading social center was the U.S.O. Club, set up in the old City Hall, now the Clatsop County Historical Society's Heritage Museum. More than one happy marriage resulted from the introduction of a local girl to an enlisted boy at a U.S.O. dance.

Scores of Clatsop County's young people

spent the war in uniform, many of them overseas. Women volunteered to become WACs, WAVES, Red Cross workers, and nurses. Hundreds of men either joined or were drafted into the service, and their deployment to distant points around the globe left parents and family burdened by worry. Astoria's Vic and Fanny Seeborg, for example, had five sons serving in the military. One of them, Arvid Seeborg, was among the 57 residents of Clatsop County who perished in World War II.

Another causality of the conflict was the heavy cruiser *Astoria*. Launched at the U.S. Naval Ship-yards on Puget Sound in 1933, the ship's sponsor was Lelia C. McKay, great granddaughter of Asto-rian Alexander McKay who lost his life on the *Tonquin*. The U.S.S. *Astoria* served the Navy proudly until August of 1942, when she was sunk during the Battle of Savo Island, taking 238 crew-men down with her.

In preparation for what was sure to be the bloody invasion of Japan, the Navy built a large hospital facility along Youngs River in 1944. The beach landings never oc-curred, but trainloads of wounded servicemen were treated at the facility before the war's end. May 8, 1945 was a joyous day across America when it was announced that Germany had surren-dered, ending the war in Europe. Three months later Japan agreed to unconditional surrender. The war was over.

Remnants of War

In the years following the war, remnants of the conflict lingered offshore. In the late 1940s, the crew of the trawler *Jimmy Boy* was not sur-prised when a barrel landed on deck along with the scads of fish falling from the net. Fishermen are accustomed to such bizarre finds. Then, one of the deckhands recognized the barnacle-encrusted barrel rolling around the deck as a depth charge. Rather than tossing it overboard for other fish-ers to find, the crew of the *Jimmy Boy* delicately hauled their catch to the Coast Guard Station at Point Adams, where on a lonely expanse of Clatsop Beach, its 300-pounds of explosives were touched off. Less fortunate were the crew of the tuna boat *Zarembo II*. Many fishermen believe that a Japanese mine carried across the ocean by the prevailing currents was responsible for removing that vessel and its occupants from the face of the Earth in 1947.

The Post War Decades
1950s - 1970s

Economic Transition

In many ways the Second World War was a high time in Astoria's history. The city's population swelled to over 25,000 and jobs were once again plentiful following the Great Depression. But this growth and prosperity was tied largely to defense spending. Just as quickly as the war boosted the community, after 1945 Astoria began a decades long backslide in both inhabitants and industry.

The economic staples that had long sustained the area continued their slow, steady decline. As Columbia River salmon runs dwindled, so too did the number of fishermen. Ocean-caught seafood kept the few remaining processing plants busy but it was nothing like it had been only a couple of generations before. In 1970, Bumble Bee Seafoods relocated its headquarters from Astoria and a decade later closed its last cannery there. In the

U.S. Representative Wendell Wyatt and his wife, Faye, pose in front of the capital building in Washington, D.C. Wyatt represented Oregon's 1st Congressional District from 1964 until 1975. (CCHS 12568.00W)

forests, too, increasingly efficient equipment and a growing reliance on smaller second-growth trees brought about a streamlined workforce. In 1989, the Astoria Plywood Mill, the city's single largest employer, shuttered its doors. The port docks greeted fewer ships and the eastbound trains departing Astoria grew shorter. With the jobs went the workers and their families.

Still, there were notable innovations in the local economy. In 1948, Wilt and Violet Paulson moved their upstart company, Lektro, Inc., into an abandoned Navy hangar at the Port of Astoria Airport. Specializing in electric-powered vehicles, the company was among the first in the nation to produce electric golf carts in 1954. The carts proved to be a strong seller for the company, outmatched only by Lektro's "electric aircraft tugs" used by airport ground crews to jockey planes on the tarmac. Introduced in 1967, the firm has installed nearly 4,000 aircraft tugs and today the device is used in airports worldwide.

Another industry that blossomed toward the end of the century was nearly as old as the city itself. In the 1970s, civic leaders began talking about incorporating tourism into the city's long-range strategy. It was far from a new idea—the Chamber of Commerce and other groups had been extolling the area's historic and scenic virtues for decades—but it met with a staunch resistance from some quarters. The shift toward tourism was gradual, but as it gained momentum the city undertook ambitious renovation projects beginning in the 1980s to spruce up the waterfront and historic downtown. The economic importance of tourism has grown steadily, and today the city is a nationally recognized tourist destination.

Health Care

In 1977, a new era in health care arrived in Astoria when Columbia Memorial Hospital opened along Exchange Street. The facility represented the most modern link in a chain of medical centers that dates back to 1880. In that year, Reverend Father Leopold Dielman purchased the Arrigoni Hotel and converted it into the town's first hospital, St. Mary's. Several newer buildings housed the Catholic-affiliated hospital, the last being a 1931 brick structure that still stands at 15th and Exchange. In 1971, St. Mary's Hospital was purchased by Columbia Hospital, a Lutheran-affiliated organization founded in 1919, which soon began laying the groundwork for a new medical center. The result was Columbia Memorial Hospital, which in the succeeding decades has continued to expand to meet the health care needs of area residents, carrying on a tradition dating back to Father Dielman.

Politics

Astoria has counted among its inhabitants a number of governors: Oswald West and Ben Olcott lived there for a time before being elected, while Robert D. Holmes and Albin W. Norblad went straight to Salem. Norblad's son, Walter,

represented Oregon's First Congressional District in the U.S. House of Representatives from 1946 until his death in 1964. In a special election held to fill the younger Norblad's seat, voters chose Astoria attorney Wendell Wyatt.

Born in Eugene in 1917, Wyatt grew up in Portland and served in the Marine Corps during the Second World War. After the conflict he moved to Astoria where he became a law partner with Albin W. Norblad. Wyatt soon became active in Oregon State Republican affairs, and after being elected to Congress in 1964, established himself as a highly respected moderate in the

party. Before leaving Congress in 1975, Wyatt served on the Interior and Appropriations committees, helped pass bills for the deepening of the Columbia River shipping channel, and supported a number of conservation projects. Wendell Wyatt continued to be an active voice in political and legal affairs nearly to his end, which came in 2009.

In city politics of the era, Harry Steinbock's name stands out. A pharmacist by trade, Steinbock served as Astoria's mayor from 1959 until 1975, and together with his wife, Mary, were involved in countless community activities. As the city's ambassadors, the Steinbocks had the privilege of welcoming presidential candidates Richard Nixon and John and Bobby Kennedy, as well as members of the Astor family. In 1963, Steinbock and others completed "sister city" arrangements with Walldorf, Germany, celebrating the occasion on the 200th birthday of Walldorf native John Jacob Astor.

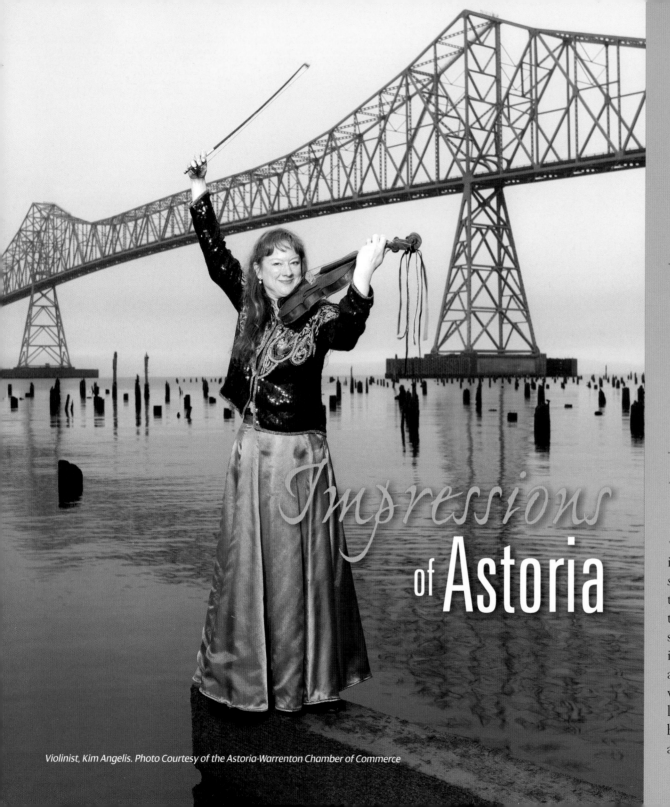

Violinist, Kim Angelis. Photo Courtesy of the Astoria-Warrenton Chamber of Commerce

The *City* Today

By Donna Quinn

"Astoria has an edge-of-the-world BEAUTY that wins your heart.

A quirky, supernatural aura hovers over it".

— *National Geographic Traveler*

You can sense it in the air, in the town, in the landscape, and in the people— history is alive in all of the disparate parts that make up today's Astoria. There is a powerful presence here, a substance, *a je ne sais quoi*, which affects those who visit or make this place their home. As Astoria evolves over time, it retains its unique character and powerful sense of place, offering deep connections to what is real and authentic. Colorful Victorian homes, a working waterfront, world-class museums, a vibrant arts community, renowned Fisher Poets, a lively Scandinavian population and a fascinating heritage create the backdrop for Astoria's thriving and diverse culture.

Like New York and San Francisco, Astoria is a gateway opened by visionary people with different ideas from the very beginning. This ongoing expansive quality allows for a "live and let live" attitude and a tolerance uncommon in communities of this size. Local historian John Goodenberger says, "There have always been oddities and eccentrics here from Day One and you can still feel their influence today." Indeed. Astoria's legendary characters continue to haunt the cracked sidewalks of the town, walking side by side with modern-day locals. There is something or someone for everyone here, and the "wabi-sabi" (a Japanese term for perfectly imperfect) element of Astoria allows people to be more fully themselves—to embrace the dark and light within them—just as the town itself does. Astoria is a curious, mysterious, and intriguing place, infused with a touch of magic and an invitation to wonder, and wander, as you discover old and new secrets.

Location

It is all about the river! The mouth of the Mighty Columbia inspired John Jacob Astor to imagine he could corner the North American fur trade from this prime location. A savvy businessman, Astor knew that capitalizing on the mouth of a huge river that connected into the interior of the country would be a brilliant move for the transport and trading of goods. Astor's vision was correct. Today, the Columbia still serves as a major maritime highway for the Northwest, and indeed our entire nation.

The river defines the town. It is a major historical character in the ongoing story of Astoria, and without it, the town would not be what it is. There is always something going on in and along the Columbia River, which attracts people of all ages and from all socio-economic walks of life—from dog walkers and joggers on the Riverwalk to skateboarders, painters, poets, families with small children, grizzled men nursing spirits from a bottle on waterfront benches, and everyday homebodies who peek out of old-fashioned windows at dusk to marvel at a fuchsia sunset that lights up the bridge and bathes the town in rainbow colors.

Jody Miller

Fifth generation Astorian and long-time mayor Willis Van Dusen says that it is the Columbia River and the Pacific Ocean which inspired the original Astoria, and it is these two magnificent water bodies that have protected its integrity today. "Like a castle surrounded by a moat, Astoria is a jewel which cannot experience urban sprawl because we are surrounded on three sides by water and the Columbia River Estuary is our front door."

The Estuary is a busy place for wildlife and for people. Trade ships still ply the waters of the Columbia as commercial and sport fishermen catch sturgeon, salmon and crab. The Astoria Yacht Club sails on Tuesdays, weather permitting. Biologists monitor and restore the rich estuary habitat as NOAA vessels conduct scientific experiments. The Coast Guard offers ongoing training within earshot of seas lions barking. Foghorns sound in the night as ships make their way to and from the Pacific Ocean.

It is this unique maritime culture that inspires journalist Joanne Rideout, who creates and produces a popular Coast Community Radio program called "The Ship Report." Each weekday, Rideout reports on international ship traffic and answers listener questions, so that the entire town knows who is on the river, what they are carrying, and the approximate time they might be passing by while exchanging bar and river pilots, day or night. At any moment one may look to the Columbia and see half a dozen huge ships anchored in front of the town, ships with names such as the "Panama Queen," "Hellenic Sky," or "Asian Pearl." The world quite literally comes to Astoria's doorstep.

The river keeps the energy moving here. One is witness to breathtaking double rainbows over roiling waters, the sun glinting off of a tugboat pulling a barge filled with golden cargo, the movement of the ships, the clouds, the river, and tides covering and uncovering old salmon cannery pil-

Jody Miller

fering soft, gentle female Yin energy in an increasingly noisy and expanding world of jangly male Yang energy. The weather builds stamina in the hardy souls who call themselves Astorians; it takes a special person to appreciate this wet bounty. In some strange way, locals who live here bond with one another because of—and perhaps in spite of—the infamous weather. Rain gives Astoria skies and days fluid movement along with rhythmic natural sounds and refreshing smells. Rain sets a mood, much like a good play, where something unexpected and interesting can happen and, in fact, in Astoria something always is.

Architecture

A recent arrival to Astoria said she was drawn to move here because "Who wouldn't want to live in a town which looks like a child designed and built it?" With a collection of brightly painted houses dotting the hillsides in random fashion and a juxtaposition of styles and various stages of upkeep, Astoria can feel like "living in a vintage postcard."

ings. All of these visual aspects create a sense that the river is offering us opportunities to pay attention to the small moments of life, to embrace the lessons of flow and the letting go that Siddhartha discovered so many centuries ago.

The Weather

Astoria has 191 days of rain and an approximate annual precipitation of almost 70 inches, making it the third wettest place in the lower 48 states. The weather helps define the character of the town and weeds out those who do not have the "sisu" (Finnish for intestinal fortitude) to persevere. Just as this town has endured for the last two

centuries, the people who live here are shaped by the weather, which is always surprising and usually welcomed, by at least some of the population.

In spite of the latest technology and frequently updated meteorological maps, the weather remains an untamed ambiguity from day to day. There is no "normal" weather in Astoria. Ferocious winter storms batter sea-going ships in front of the town and shred banners hanging on downtown streetlights. Winter rain does not just fall down straight from the sky, it whistles in with a wind that blows the drops horizontal drenching you in seconds, with or without an umbrella. Keeps you in the present, that!

Rain makes Astoria an introspective place, of-

"Astoria is definitely not cutesy," says Historian John Goodenberger, who was born in Astoria and decided to move back after experiencing big cities. "I returned to Astoria because everything I wanted was here: the size, the

Jody Miller

people, the history, the buildings. In Astoria, change has been slow to happen, which has been a benefit. It did not all come in at once—it was gradual—you can still recognize the town. I came back because of the arts, culture, and preservation. In the 1980s it was really a gritty place with strip bars downtown and what not. Even though we lost some great old buildings in the 1960s, we still have a lot of architectural integrity. You can round a corner here and be in 1925. This is a very real place, not a faux or precious town."

Astoria has mid to late 19th century and early 20th century architecture with the largest stock of pre-1950 houses per capita of any town in Oregon. Within two downtown National Register Historic Districts are Gothic Revival, Queen Anne and Italianate Victorians, Colonial Revival and Tudor Revival, Prairie School and Craftsman homes. The charming collection of pre-Victorian, Victorian, and Craftsman houses are made of wood, reflecting the construction materials of the area. All the canneries were big wooden structures over wood pilings in the river. There is a vernacular (or low style functional) and industrial architectural style that was passed on from generation to generation. Some locals simply refer to these homes as "fishermen's cottages."

The human scale retro-downtown is virtually all from the same era because of the great fire of 1922. Almost all buildings downtown were built between 1923 and 1925. This makes Asto-

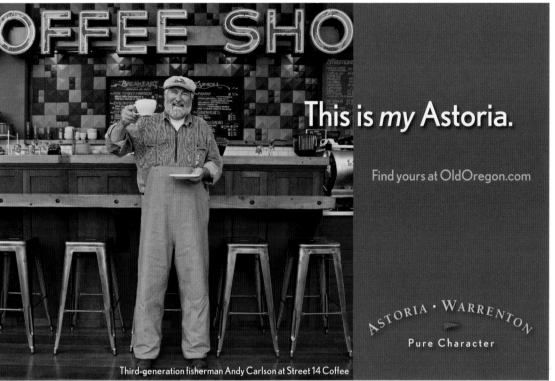

This is *my* Astoria.

Find yours at OldOregon.com

ASTORIA · WARRENTON
Pure Character

Third-generation fisherman Andy Carlson at Street 14 Coffee

ria's downtown a real period piece—hard to find in today's world. The neighborhoods reflect some evolution and gradual buildings of different styles in some places, but downtown remains virtually the same as it was in the 1920s—a huge gift—a living museum, authentic and functional at the same time.

Astoria has an underground that is not open to the public because it is "an unusual sort of place." Goodenberger says that Astoria's underground was a response to building the town over a former wetlands. "In 1915 people realized the town was too close to the water, so downtown was raised 4 feet to get it out of the swamp, which gave stores full basements. It was done for structure but it is a real curiosity. What you would see in the underground would be bases of buildings and pipes

and long tunnels of concrete." As locals and visitors explore Astoria's downtown, they may notice squares with colored glass bricks embedded in the sidewalks. These bricks let light into the underground. It is thought that they were originally clear, but with age, they have become the beautiful shade of purple they are today.

Artists like Sally Lackaff are passionate about "the old decrepit feel of the town" which somehow seems to meld nicely with the ongoing renaissance of the downtown core. While some may consider old buildings in a state of disrepair "blight," others relish them as part of Astoria's history and gritty past. As high-end art galleries and new eateries nestle next to shabby buildings, elements which may seem at first impossible to work together do. The old, the worn, the weathered, and the respectfully restored contribute to the "real" in Astoria.

While visitors to Astoria love the iconic attractions such as the Astoria Column, the Riverfront Trolley, the museums, and other tourist must-see's, they truly adore Astoria's neighborhoods with charming streets, hidden trails, strange staircases, verdant gardens, and the colorful, highly individual historic homes with quirky trim and fanciful flourishes. Steve Forrester, publisher of the local newspaper *The Daily Astorian,* often refers to Astoria as a "living museum," "a museum without walls," and "a giant attic" where one could find almost anything. And one can.

Arts & Culture

Astoria attracts larger-than-life characters, following in the tradition of the city's founder and the early settlers. It is populated by unorthodox and unconventional wanderers, adventurers, vagabonds, and freethinkers as well as a few normal folks. And, because of its tolerance for diversity, everyone seems to find a niche. There are Astorians by birth, by chance, and by choice, and all of them discover and rediscover something they need here, something only this place seems to offer.

Astoria Coffee House owner Jim DeFeo moved to Astoria because he and his partner both liked the Bohemian mentality they feel exists in the town. "There are a lot of people here who like gathering places that are esthetically pleasing. Astoria is not the 9 to 5 crowd, it's the non-corporate counter culture, a place where philosophers, artists, poets and musicians hang out. Of course there are regular joes who come in for a latte and the New York Times; Astoria is a place where everyone feels comfortable, like they belong. It's a real mixture of ages, an evolving of young and old—not just people who want to grab lunch and check their emails—they really want to connect with other folks."

One way locals connect is through philanthropy. There are many non-profit organizations here, and Astorians support them with benefits, concerts, and poetry readings. DeFeo observes that "the creative class of people are the people making

Jody Miller

the difference here today, they're flourishing. This town has soul, and being by the water is a very spiritual thing too. It's an exciting time in Astoria, because there's definitely a renaissance going on. We're still pioneers in Astoria after 200 years!"

A generous spirit of volunteerism really makes Astoria work. Judy Niland, Managing Director of the Astor Street Opry Company, figures that if newcomers can respect who and what is already here, and if they are willing to participate in the community, then Astoria will make a place for them. "People are not judged on appearance,

possessions or educational background here. The rough edges of this town allow people to be themselves without pretense."

Some of these volunteers turn out to help the Astor Street Opry Company put on its annual summer melodrama "Shanghaied in Astoria." Performed in vaudeville style, this popular production helps preserve regional folklore and celebrate Astoria's culture. "Shanghaied is part of cultural tourism. It tells the story of the fishing and cannery life here," says Judy Niland.

Only in Astoria does the annual Fisher Poets Gathering take place. Since 1998, inspired fishermen and women from Alaska and the Pacific Northwest have traveled to Astoria for the now nationally famous gathering, where poets and singers tell tales that honor the fishing industry and lifestyle. The Fisher Poet's Gathering has become a highlight among Astoria's many cultural happenings and has been lauded in the *New York Times*, along with other national and international publications. Local Fisherman-Poet Dave Densmore says "Astoria's strongest defining feature today is the awareness of her place in and importance of the surrounding natural world."

Astoria is a port of call for cruise ships whose passengers enjoy the thriving Sunday Market, the second largest in the state. The Astoria-Warrenton Chamber sponsors a yearly Crab and Seafood Festival. A Great Columbia Crossing event allows people from all over the world to walk or run across the Astoria-Megler Bridge, which is closed

to cars for just a few hours once a year in the fall for this festive occasion. There is an Astoria International Film Festival, a Scandinavian Midsummer Festival, a Commercial Fisherman's Festival, and the world-class Astoria Music Festival featuring opera and classical divas from New York and Europe.

Astorians are well aware that it is their town's authenticity that makes this all work. People like Robert "Jake" Jacob, who was born in Astoria and created the luxury boutique Cannery Pier Hotel over the Columbia River, want to ensure that "spaghetti does not become pasta, coffee does not become lattes, and junk does not become antiques"—all signs Jacob feels that a town is

becoming a bit too yuppified to retain its original essence.

Fins, Finns & Astorians author Greg Jacob grew up in Astoria listening to the sound of fog horns and the squeak and groan of old pilings as the tide ebbed and flowed. "You can still experience this in Astoria today. The town hasn't been paved over yet and there are ongoing events which connect Astoria with its Scandinavian heritage. The ethnic character of this place provides a nice mix of craziness, which is part of Astoria's charm."

That charm is well represented in Astoria's one-of-a-kind venues. The Voodoo Room offers local musicians, like the Brownsmead Flats and the Bond Street Blues Band, a funky and eclectic place to play. The adjacent Columbian Theatre has great pizzas, beer, and wine to imbibe as you watch a classic film or a live theatrical presentation. The award-winning and magnificently restored Liberty Theater has a cultural offerings calendar that would be impressive in any major city. Famous performers and touring musicians delight in performing in the Liberty, which has been compared to the great opera houses of Europe.

Astoria has a more culturally diverse population than most small towns of 10,000. Veterans and peaceniks face off on Fridays in front of the Astoria Post Office and on Marine Drive. Finns, Danes, Swedes, and Norwegians all patronize Finn Ware, a Finnish curio shop downtown, and sing along with local radio show, "The Scandinavian Hour" on Saturday afternoons. Metaphysical healing circles meet in former bars and brothels downtown as Clatsop Community College professors offer chemistry, philosophy, and yoga classes on the hill. The Astoria Fiber Arts Academy teaches spinning on old-fashioned looms, while

in the next block tattoo artists beckon. The Blue Scorcher Bakery and Café offers vegan cuisine and "grow local, eat local" workshops while the landmark Mary Todd's Workers Bar and Grill (in business since 1924) offers a chance to be part of a different kind of local scene.

It all happens in this remarkable little town made famous because of its history, a town now treasured for maintaining its "pure character" even as it evolves with time. It is a place that has attracted national attention because of its singular qualities, where circumscribed generic mediocrity and theme park artifice do not exist.

Today, Astoria's rich past remains a colorful tapestry that weaves this living legend of the American West in a magical aura—its presence is palpable in the thick salt air that wraps itself around the Victorian homes that cling to steep hillsides, and the aging cannery pilings which speak of a bygone era. The elements of wonder and surprise continue to exist in this inscrutable place called Astoria. Spirits of long ago explorers and fisherman are still here in the River, the old ones say. They are watching over this place, reminding us that we must continue to persevere, to live with "sisu," here at the edge of the world, here in elusive, enigmatic, mysterious, and altogether amazing Astoria, Oregon.

LIBERTY THEATER
Our Community Treasure
By Rosemary Baker-Monaghan, Executive Director

The highest and best expression of the human mind and spirit is achieved through the Arts.

Those of us who call northwest Oregon and southwest Washington home realize we are blessed to live in an area with so many treasures that enrich our lives. We enjoy unsurpassed scenic beauty and many great community organizations that work hard to improve our quality of life. The Liberty Theater is one of these treasures.

When the Liberty Theater opened in 1925, Astoria was still rebuilding from the Great Fire that had devastated the city three years before. The new building stood on the site of the Weinhard Astoria Hotel, one of the most lavish structures destroyed by the fire. The hotel had been built as a showplace with dark oak paneling throughout, Belgian carpets, and custom furnishings. Today, the Liberty's stage is located near where the front desk stood as it faced the hotel's main entrance on Duane Street.

A group of Seattle and Portland investors closed a deal on the city block where the Liberty now stands in May 1924. They hired the Portland architectural firm of Bennes and Herzog to draw plans for a "super modern structure" consisting of stores, office rooms, and a 1,000-seat theater. The complex was to be of "Italianate design" different from any structure north of Los Angeles, with "an ornamental loggia to run about the entirety of the building."

Jensen and Von Herberg signed on to equip and run the theater, pledging $60,000 to "fit the theater in the most elegant style according to the best business practice." The surviving portion of the Weinhard Astoria Hotel's foundation was used as the base of the new building. Once finished, the *Astoria Evening Budget* described The Liberty Theater as the "most artistic and comfortable theater in the West".

The Liberty Theater opened on April 4, 1925. Designated as a Class A Vaudeville House, shows began at 1:30 p.m. and ran continuously into the night. Admission was twenty-five cents and candy could be purchased outside at the adjoining newsstand. In addition to the theater, the structure housed a radio station, a dance studio, and about two-dozen businesses. From its inception, the Liberty Theater Complex became the centerpiece of economic, cultural, and social activity, and a part of the heart and soul of our community.

Over the next seven decades the Liberty Theater enjoyed a rich and full history. By the 1990s though, the grand old girl was in tough shape. Liberty Restoration Inc., a non-profit organization, purchased the entire block in 1998 and began restoration. To date, two phases of a three-phase restoration project have been completed. Costing roughly $8.9 million dollars, the funds have been generously donated by many individuals and foundations. Remaining restoration projects include the back stage area, second floor space along 12th and Duane, areas for dressing, rehearsal, and classrooms, a new sound system, and a business office.

The Liberty Theater represents what a community can do when it comes together for a common purpose. Over the past decade our stage has hosted events that reach a broad range of audiences including festivals celebrating different cultures and ethnicities, community concerts from country to rock, music festivals featuring classical and operatic presentations, forums dealing with local and national issues, Clatsop Community College's graduation ceremony, weddings, and children's theater. The Liberty Theater is truly a community treasure.

Trolley Tracks Through Time

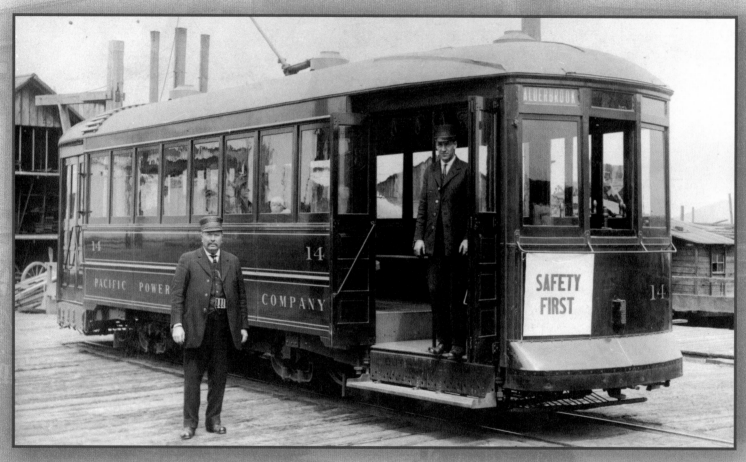

It only costs a dollar to take a ride back in history.

At least that is the case in Astoria, where that modest fare gets passengers onboard the vintage trolley Old 300 as it rolls along the waterfront from Uniontown to Uppertown and back. The rhythmic clickety-clack of steel on steel hearkens back to a time when the bustle of streetcars was part of the everyday scene. Along the route, Old 300's conductors provide a running narrative that brings riders ever closer to the bygone days of the old town and majestic river, as the two blend beneath the rails.

The American Car Company of St. Louis built what would come to be known as Old 300 for a streetcar line in San Antonio, Texas. That was in 1913, the same year that American turned out three new trolleys for Astoria's street railway and its new franchisees: the Pacific Power & Light Company.

By 1913, the city's streetcar system was already a quarter of a century old. Back in 1888, the first segment of the line connected Uppertown with the downtown area via a wooden causeway spanning Scow Bay that would become Exchange Street. Three small coaches, each pulled by a horse, ferried the first passengers across town from what is now 7th Street to 31st Street. The trip cost a nickel. As the business grew so did the number of cars and the service area.

Electrification of the line came in 1891 when workers installed a power plant in Uppertown, strung wires above the tracks, and converted the horse-drawn cars into trolleys. Financial problems plagued the Astoria Street Railway Company over the ensuing decade, and it eventually ended up as part of General Electric, the firm that had provided the equipment to electrify the line to begin with. Despite the economic upheaval, by 1904 the rails reached east to Alderbrook.

Pacific Power & Light took over the street railway in 1910—along with Astoria's electric light plant and gas works—and would operate it until the proverbial end of the line in 1924. But before that unfortunate day, P. P. & L continued expanding the line westward, reaching Taylor's Addition on Alameda Avenue in 1915. They also raised the old nickel fare to seven cents.

Then, on December 8, 1922, the commercial district of Astoria was leveled by a great inferno. In addition to razing 32 city blocks, the Great Fire destroyed the streetcar line on Commercial and Bond streets, leaving the steel rails a heat-twisted ruin. The trolleys, which spent that wicked night safely housed in the car barn, could go no further east then 10th Street—the western extreme of the fire. Several streetcars were later shipped to

the east side of the burnt district to resume service between 17th and 45th streets, but the Great Fire had cut the line in two.

During reconstruction the city commission required that P. P. & L. pave the streets that were to carry its rebuilt tracks. It was a cost the electric company could hardly justify. Astoria's street railway had been operating in the red for a number of years, and in early 1924, P. P. & L. put the line up

Roger Warren

for sale. Municipal officials saw the trolley system as out of step with the modernity of the new city that was taking shape. The future, they declared, lay with motorbuses. On June 29, 1924, the streetcars made their final run.

Nine years after trolley service came to an end in Astoria, Old 300 was taken off its run in

San Antonio and placed outside a local museum. In the decades to follow, the coach occasionally received new paint and superficial repairs but little substantive restoration work was done until 1980. Old 300 eventually found its way to Portland and then in 1998 to Astoria where volunteers overhauled the trolley. In 2006, the city purchased the Old 300 from the San Antonio Museum Association, but by then it had already become a waterfront institution.

Today, volunteers with The Astoria Riverfront Trolley Association care for and operate Old 300. From late spring through the fall, the streetcar clatters along its nearly three-mile route from the West Mooring Basin to the foot of 39th Street.

The Astoria Column

Among the area's iconic structures, the Astoria Column stands above the rest.

Rising from the crest of Coxcomb Hill, the 125-foot Column is an unmistakable beacon crowning the cityscape. Countless visitors have ascended the 164 spiraling stair steps within the structure to the observation platform, where they have been rewarded with an unparalleled vista of the lower Columbia River estuary and Coast Range mountains.

The Column's origins can be traced back to St. Paul, Minnesota. This unlikeliest of birthplaces happened to be the home of Ralph Budd, president of the Great Northern Railway, who took it upon himself to have historical monuments placed along his company's line. Astoria, he announced in 1925, would be the site of a permanent memorial to three remarkable events in Western history: Captain Robert Gray's "discovery" of the Columbia River, the Lewis & Clark Expedition, and the founding of the first American settlement west of the Rocky Mountains.

Budd engaged New York architect Electus D. Litchfield to design the monument. Litchfield's plans called for a 150-foot cement tower that would be adorned with bas-relief engravings depicting the historical epochs. Vincent Astor, the great grandson of Astoria's namesake, was enlisted to help finance the ambitious project. As the plan matured, Budd and Litchfield selected Italian-born artist Attilio Pusterla to create the Column's exterior artwork.

It was agreed from an early date that Coxcomb Hill, the highest point on the Astoria peninsula, would be the ideal location for the monument. The 30-acre site had lingered as part of the city's parks program since it was acquired with funds left over from the Centennial Celebration of 1911. Even before the promontory became city property, some Astorians had proposed locating an observatory there, but differing opinions and financial concerns stonewalled the plans.

One of the early and ardent supporters for a historical monument on the hill was local logger John Chitwood. Sometimes called "The Father of Coxcomb Hill," Chitwood's paternal connection came from the pioneer trail he hacked to the summit in the late 1800s. There, he declared to anyone who would listen, should be located a monument to all trailblazers that had come before. In 1917, the 78-year-old Chitwood realized some portion of his dream when a young Finn in his employ transformed a hilltop spruce tree into an enormous flagpole. Unfortunately, six years later the limbless trunk was struck by lightning and destroyed.

Construction began on the Astoria Column on April Fool's Day 1926. According to Column historian Joean K. Fransen, once the 12-foot deep foundation concrete was poured, contractors made rapid upward progress adding some 9 feet to the shaft per day. From Litchfield's original plans the Column had been scaled back to 125 feet in height, which workmen reached by June.

On July 1, 1926, Attilio Pusterla went to work on the pictorial friezes.

The artwork was done using the "sgraffito" method, which Astorians were quick to learn, was a classic Italian medium that combined carving and painting. The Column was first painted with an undercoat of brown and then covered in white plaster which, when chiseled away, gave form to the figures. Working from his scaffolding, Pusterla completed the last of his 14 scenes at the end of October, nearly three months after the formal dedication ceremony.

Ralph Budd set July 22, 1926 as the Column's official opening, and despite Pusterla's continuing work, went ahead with the ceremonies. Dignitaries from across the nation arrived in Astoria to revel in three days of speeches, pageants, parades, and feasting. Once complete the Astoria Column was given to the city.

The coastal weather soon began to take its toll on the monument. Unable to pay for the necessary repairs to Pusterla's work, the City of Astoria began to search for assistance. Financial help came from the Astor family and the Great Northern Railroad. In 1935, the aged Pusterla mounted the scaffolding once more to touch up his original friezes.

In 1988, the non-profit Friends of the Astoria Column was founded, and none too soon. In the 1960s and 1970s, the Column received badly needed structural upgrades, but by the 1980s the sgraffito scenes were again showing wear. In 1995, the group raised money to refurbish the exterior and nine years later spearheaded the renovation of the monument's plaza. To this day, the Friends of the Astoria Column continues its work preserving the historic monument which, according to the Astoria-Warrenton Area Chamber of Commerce, receives over 400,000 visitors annually.

Is it the Astor Column or Astoria Column?

Over the years some confusion has arisen over the name of the monument on top of Coxcomb Hill. In its early days it was called the "Astor Column." That was the title given to the 1927 pamphlet published by the Astoria Chamber of Commerce first describing the new structure. And there is valid reason for the epithet. Monies donated by the Astor family helped pay for the land upon which the monument sits, its construction, and once for its upkeep. In more recent times, however, it has become known as the "Astoria Column," a name that pays equal homage to the historical events that the monument celebrates.

Spanning the Columbia
THE ASTORIA-MEGLER BRIDGE

By Luke Wirkkala

Today, the steel and concrete giant is a fixture of the Astoria skyline, and hard to imagine not being there. But building the bridge was far from an easy task, and one that required perseverance from proponents in both Washington and Oregon for decades.

There had long been talk of building a bridge on the lower Columbia, but the first serious effort to make it a reality did not come until the 1930s. A group called the Oregon-Washington Bridge Trustees worked to garner funding for the project through President Franklin Roosevelt's Public Works Administration. Due largely to the trustees' efforts, Congress passed a bill in 1934 that authorized construction of a toll bridge at Astoria for an estimated cost of $6 million. Unfortunately, monies did not materialize and the next major step forward would not occur for another two decades, as action was stalled by debate, deliberation, and the wartime turmoil of the 1940s.

In 1953, the Port of Astoria organized a $50,000 bridge feasibility study. It was concluded that a bridge could be constructed for $25,400,000, though it would be a matter to be decided by the legislatures of Oregon and Washington. Oregon passed the bill in 1959, and two years later, Washington followed suit.

Washington State engineer William A. Bugee was hired to design the 4.1-mile bridge, which would connect Astoria to Point Ellice, Washington. Close to 12,000 feet of that length was to be a viaduct that would cross Desdemona Sands mid-river at an elevation of 25 feet. Near the Washington shore, a superstructure would lift the highway 49 feet above the river, and to the south, a span of 2,464 feet would rise 200 feet above the main shipping channel. To this day, this section of bridge remains the longest three-span, continuous cantilever through-truss in the world.

Construction began in August 1962, when Oregon Governor Mark Hatfield used a golden shovel to dig the first ceremonial scoop of earth in Astoria. The next step was to sink hollow, bell-shaped forms (cast at Tongue Point) to the river bottom and fill them with concrete. The deepest of these 32 pier foundations sit at 85 feet below mean water level, with some of the foundation pile extending down as far as 190 feet below the riverbed.

Like the bridge's concrete piers, the steel superstructure was prefabricated and then barged to site, though in this case, the components traveled from Vancouver, Washington. The American Bridge Division of U.S. Steel Corporation was responsible for construction of the superstructure, and they employed special jack-up barges to lift the immense bridge sections into place, some of which weighed as much as 840 tons. The middle, viaduct section of the bridge was completed

almost entirely by barge. But after the final section of bridge was put into place, concrete work still remained on the high steel.

In May of 1963 a project manager named George Bauer was killed when a support cable snapped and knocked him into the river. This was the only fatality that occurred during construction, but there were several close calls and two serious accidents. Erick Lukkarinen of Astoria fell 40 feet to a dirt trail, breaking his knee and shoulder. Gary Foss of Gearhart took a 20-foot drop to a concrete floor pier, broke his back, and was left paralyzed.

The Astoria-Megler Bridge opened to one-lane traffic on July 29, 1966, and was formally dedicated on August 27. On that day, Governor Hatfield and Washington Governor Daniel Evans were there with Miss Washington, Sandra Lee Marth, and Miss Oregon, Estrellita Schiel, for a ribbon cutting ceremony as a crowd of more than 30,000 people looked on.

Over 400,000 vehicles crossed the bridge in the first full year of operation, far exceeding even the most optimistic of projections. While under construction, critics had called the bridge a white elephant and labeled it "the bridge to nowhere." But time has proven them wrong. In 1993, the

bridge had paid for itself through its toll charge, more than two years early, and today more than 1 million vehicles make the crossing each year.

Perhaps even more impressive than the use the bridge has seen is the engineering that made its construction possible. "We did all sorts of spectacular things here and were either tremendously successful or fabulously lucky," said project engineer Robert Cunningham. "We couldn't put a tape measure out in the water and measure how long that main span was going to be, we had to sit here on the bank and figure it by triangulation. But for that 2,460-foot span, we were off by five-eighths of an inch."

FREE WILLY

HOW FAR WOULD YOU GO FOR A FRIEND?

Images Courtesy of the Oregon Film Museum

The Hollywood of the Northwest

Why Cinemaphiles Love Astoria

By Donna Quinn

Filmmakers have been seduced by Astoria's stunning geography, historic buildings, and original character since the first major commercial motion picture, "The Fisherman's Bride," was shot here in 1908. Since then Astoria has attracted Hollywood scouts, movie stars, filmmakers, and fans from all over the world. Just shout "Goonies Never Say Die!" on a crowded street in Japan and see what happens.

Astoria's fame as a favored film location has made it an international destination for enthusiastic fans of "Kindergarten Cop," "Free Willy," "Short Circuit," and "The Goonies" who want to experience Astoria's magic for themselves, and pay homage to revered film sites with friends and family. Nearly every season someone is filming in Astoria, whether independent filmmakers, Hollywood moguls, or Gen-X'ers making YouTube videos with their cell phones. It's just that kind of town. People have been trying to capture Astoria's *je ne sais quoi* on film for over a hundred years.

Now Astoria boasts the only museum in the state dedicated to preserving and celebrating the art and legacy of films and filmmaking in Oregon. Although the Oregon Film Museum, located in the picturesque 1914 Clatsop County Jail, offers a map showing the locations of over 300 films that have been made in Oregon, Astoria reigns as a crown jewel.

While Lewis & Clark's Journey of Discovery initially made the Columbia-Pacific region an internationally recognized spot on the global map, these days Astoria's renown for the movies filmed here reverberates in almost every language and in every country. Tourists flock to the Chamber of Commerce to get the address of "The Goonies" house and find out how to take a self-guided movie location tour.

All Images Courtesy of the Oregon Film Museum

The 25th anniversary of "The Goonies" in June of 2010 brought people from all over the world who wanted to meet the stars and see their favorite film shown in the magnificently restored Liberty Theatre, and in the funky and fun Columbian Theatre where you can drink beer or wine in the balcony while enjoying a Voodoo Lounge homemade pizza.

Clatsop County Historical Society Executive Director McAndrew Burns reflects on Astoria's stature as a filmmaker's paradise: ''Hollywood loves authenticity, and we have that here, along with a certain intrigue and mystery because of our 'wild' history. When you consider the natural elements which exist here, along with our incredible architecture, and then add in our changeable and exciting weather, our iconic attractions such as the Astoria-Megler Bridge and the Astoria Column with its views out to the Graveyard of the Pacific, well, you just can't find all those things anywhere else."

Fifth Generation Astorian, Mayor Willis Van Dusen, who had a speaking part in "Free Willy," says that Astoria's beautiful location perched above the Columbia River Estuary provides a constantly changing background canvas of motion, light, shadow, texture, and perspective which filmmakers appreciate. All good reasons why Astoria has been the location of over a dozen well-known movies, including "Into The Wild," "Benji," "The Guardian," "Come See The Paradise," "Teenage Mutant Ninja Turtles III," "The Ring II," and multiple documentaries, including a short documentary, "Astoria, Oregon: An Adventure in History" produced by the Clatsop County Historical Society to help commemorate Astoria's Bicentennial. The Astoria International Film Festival takes place at The Liberty Theater each fall and there is always an Astoria film in the line-up.

Just as Hollywood fell in love with Astoria, Clark Gable fell in love with a young woman when he began his acting career here in 1922 at the Astoria Theatre. A plaque at 12th Street and Duane commemorates the site of this momentous occasion. Gable went on to become the "King of Hollywood" and there are still some old-timers around who remember their twitterpatted mothers talking about encounters with Gable while he was here.

Today local Astorians take drinking, dancing, or fishing with the stars and being extras in a wide range of films in stride—it's just the norm (if there is such a thing in Astoria). Most folks on the street will smile at you if you ask them where a certain movie location can be found, and they'll usually point you in the right direction. No matter where you go in Astoria though, there's always a shot that would be right for a movie somewhere. Lights, camera, action, and Roll On Astoria! For the 'Hollywood of the Northwest,' every day here is the real deal, and that translates into some pretty fine fantasies on film, with or without sunglasses. Movies after all are about compelling stories and images, and Astoria is the ... CUT ... and that's a wrap!

NW Natural®

We grew up here.

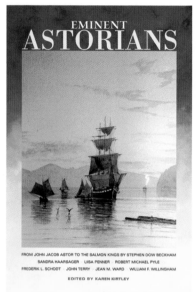

100 years of service to the community. And counting.

At Pacific Power, we've provided a simple, essential service for a century: lighting cities and warming homes. Our dedicated service to local communities has been the foundation of our 100-year history.

 PACIFIC POWER

Let's turn the answers on.